Off the RACE Track

...From Color-Blind to ...Color-Kind

by Steve Simms

Off the RACE Track

. . .

From Color-Blind to Color-Kind

By Steve Simms

Beyond Books
Nashville, Tennessee

Off the RACE Track...From Color-Blind to Color-Kind

BEYOND BOOKS...
NASHVILLE, TENNESSEE
PRINTED IN THE UNITED STATES OF AMERICA

Author's Page:
https://www.amazon.com/Steve-Simms/e/B019IPIY3W

© COPYRIGHT STEVE SIMMS, 2018

Editing Assistance by Douglas W. Krieger, Editor, Tribnet Publications

ISBN: 9781726663885

EXTERIOR COVER DESIGN BY DOUGLAS W. KRIEGER

All contents are original (except for the quotations) -- All rights reserved solely by the author (Steve Simms). The author guarantees all contents are original and do not infringe upon the legal rights of any other person or work. No part of this book may be reproduced in any form without the permission of the author. The views expressed in this book are those of the publisher/author.

ALL SCRIPTURE TAKEN FROM THE NIV—NEW INTERNATIONAL VERSION OF THE BIBLE UNLESS OTHERWISE NOTED

Table of Contents

1. *Race Forward?* *1*
   - Starting with a Haircut from Oprah Winfrey's Dad 2
   - Vernon Winfrey–# 1 Barber in Tennessee. 4
   - 5 Colorful People & A Drab, Gray Elephant in A Dark Room 6
   - The Treasure of Me and My Color 9
   - Cross-Color Builders Experience the Treasure of Color 12
   - Hop Along With Me 15
   - Am I Out Of Step With Truth? 16
   - What Color Is A Human Kidney? 17

2. *From Colorblind to Color Appreciation* *21*
   - Saying Fresh Things in New Ways 21
   - My Story 22
   - Alternative View Of Color 30
   - More About My Struggles with My Own Colorblindness 32
   - Cross-Walking In Paducah, Kentucky 33
   - COGIC 35
   - White Guy on The Streets in The Hood 38
   - Ernie's Surprise Experience of Discrimination 42
   - The Salvation Army 43
   - Bob's Racial Trauma 46
   - Salvation Army Inner City Community Center 47
   - Starting A Salvation Army Church in The Hood 50
   - Back to 1957 Again 52
   - A Sad Ending to Our Multi-Racial Community 53
   - So Many Friends 55

3. *My Top 10 Greatest Americans* *57*
   - American Greatness and The People Under the Skin! 57
   - Two of My 21st Century American Heroes 82

4. *Early Jewish, Christian, Jesus' Views on Race* *87*

Table of Contents

More of My Original Thinking About Race 87

Ancient Views of Skin Color 87

The Jewish Version Colorblind Racism 88

White as a Sheet Full of Animals 91

Early *Gracist* Community of Reconciliation & Unity 93

Questions for Civil Rights Leader, Ralph Abernathy 95

America's Divided Churches 96

Torah-fying For Healing? 98

5. *Short History on White/Black Interaction* *103*

Some of My Original Thoughts About History 103

Black History Is American History 104

Why A White Guy Digs into Black History 104

Black and White 106

A Light Upon America's Colorful History of Slavery? 107

How did Slavery Start in the USA? 108

Definition of Blackness 110

Today's Definition of Blackness 116

Curse of Ham? 118

Civil War Between the States 122

Southerners in The Union Army 124

What About After Slavery? 125

Civil Rights Movement 131

Freedom Riders of The Civil Rights Movement 132

Monteagle, Tennessee Civil Rights Movement 135

Selma 137

Stages of Racism in America 138

6. *Skin Colors—Plantations—Chattanooga* *139*

Original Skin Color Thoughts 139

Belle Meade Plantation 142

Travellers Rest Plantation 145

Andrew Jackson's Hermitage & Slave Life 148

Definition of Plantation 154

Table of Contents

    Antebellum: Pre-Civil War. 155

    Vacationing in Chattanooga, Tennessee 156

7. *The Meaning of Dr. King's Dream? 161*

    Creatively Thinking About Color-Kindness 161

    King's Dream of Not Being Judged by Color 162

    Eye-Color-Blindness 163

    Time for Color-Appreciation 164

    Color-Kindness Challenge 166

    A Few Kindness Quotes and Comments 168

    Color-Blindness Quotes and Comments 169

    Fun Skin Facts Cultivating Skin-Color-Appreciation 172

8. *Heroes of Liberty & Justice for All 177*

    More Original Thoughts 177

    Remembering an American Atrocity 177

    Tennessee's Abolitionist Newspaper 179

    America's Forgotten Freedom Fighters 181

    Frederick Douglas 183

    Sojourner Truth 185

    Uncle Tom's Cabin by Harriet Beecher Stowe 186

    Black Like Me by John Howard Griffin 189

    Pudd'nhead Wilson, by Mark Twain 190

    James McCune Smith 192

    Am I Related to American Hero, William Simms? 194

9. *Leaving the Lie: Blackness, Being Unracist 197*

    Race Comments Never Said Like This Before 197

    Refuting America's Big Lie About Blackness 197

    You Might be Unracist IF… 199

    Racial Reconciliation in the 1800s 201

    A 3rd Grade Lesson on Racism through EYES 205

    My Own Blue Eyes 209

    A Myth That Needs to Go 210

Table of Contents

    USA Government's Confusing "Racial" Categories 211

    Alternative to Skin-Color Categorization – DISC 213

10. *Cash for Slaves & Priceless Courage* *217*

    More of My Innovative Thoughts About Race 217

    America's Forgotten Black *Trail Of Tears* 217

    Charles Ball's Personal Account of Slavery 221

    Was Jesus Whipped in America? 222

    Negro Spirituals 225

    Quotes from Quobna Ottobah Cugoano 226

    Prime Shipping in Mr. Brown's Box 228

    Underground Railroad 230

11. *Seeing More Clearly?* *233*

    Fresh Thoughts About Race 233

    Blame and Shame 234

    Shoots and Roots 235

    Injustice Hidden Behind the Bill Of Rights 236

    First Amendment for White Americans: 237

    Dodging Slavery And Racial Injustice? 243

    Common Pictures In American Wallets & Purses 246

    After Charleston Black Church Shooting? 248

    Apology 252

    Say it: "Black Lives Matter" & Why? 255

    Practical Steps to Color-Kindness 255

12. *A Few Encouraging Quotes* *263*

REVIEWS *266*

Table of Contents

1. Race Forward?

Winfrey's Barber Shop; Bridge Building; Frog Legs; The Treasure of Me, Rhythm, And Inner Color

Let's explore three questions about America's color disconnection. Where did it come from? Why is it such an ongoing problem? And, can we overcome it?

I love color and can't imagine life without it. Color beautifies the world around us. Dare we be open? Color also beautifies people!

There is much greatness in every shade of human being; however, too often we cannot see the greatness for color's intrusion. Skin color has never been a problem in America, however, sadly, our negative definitions of skin color have released centuries of pain, suffering, guilt, and shame on all colors of Americans. Skin color is real, but perhaps race, meaning major differences based on skin color, is not real.

The attitudes and beliefs that keep colors apart in America breed hostility and prevent us from being a united collage of human hearts. We like to label in-groups and out-groups, but everywhere I look, I see colorful shades of the human group.

I have been personally exploring the joy of human color in America for decades, especially black and white relationships. (I share more about that in chapter 3) I have actually become an inverse paranoid when it comes to color. I view people of every skin hue as people who want to do good things for me, who want to befriend me. And I want to get to know them better.

So, come along with me and let me share some of the experiences, knowledge, fun, relationships, and insights I have gained in my journey from color-apathy to color-appreciation.

Starting with a Haircut from Oprah Winfrey's Dad

"Get a haircut from Vernon Winfrey," for weeks that thought kept going through my head—and it frightened me. I am a white guy and I had never had a haircut in a black barber shop. Mr. Winfrey is the father of now famed Oprah Winfrey and runs a barber shop in East Nashville.

Deciding to act on this strange "leading," I called Winfrey's Barber Shop. He answered. I asked how much a haircut was. He said ten dollars. I said I would be there soon. I got on the internet, found the directions, then drove to his shop. As I turned on Vernon Winfrey Avenue, my throat felt dry. I saw the shop. There was Mr. Winfrey standing outside with several other men. I felt panic and drove out of the neighborhood. The next morning, I got a haircut at my usual place.

"At least I tried," I thought. But I knew—I had "chickened out"—and was going to have to go back when my hair grew out. So why was I so afraid? I didn't fear physical harm—although I remembered how those courageous black people who integrated lunch counters in the early 1960s were treated—those folks were real heroes. All I was being prompted to do was get a haircut in the Twenty-First Century.

A few weeks later, I drove to Mr. Winfrey's shop again, with a determination to succeed. Fortunately, no one was standing outside when I got there. There was a parking space by the door. I parked, jumped out and rushed into the shop, before I could even think about what I was doing.

My abrupt entry startled me. The building was small. Three barber chairs were to my right and Vernon was standing behind the first one cutting a 12-year-old's hair. Five men were in the waiting area.

I glanced around and then stared at Mr. Winfrey who had stopped cutting and was staring back at me. No one spoke. I could feel my heart pounding.

Finally, I got some words out:

"I, uh, would, uh, (pause) like to, uh, get a haircut."

"Sure, take a seat," he replied.

"I've got to be somewhere in an hour," I said. "Can you get me before then?"

"I can't get you in an hour," he said.

Whew, did I feel relieved–for about two seconds–until the thought popped in my head, "Ask if he can get to you tomorrow." I got those words out and Vernon said tomorrow would be better for him because he wouldn't be so crowded.

"Ok," I said, "See you tomorrow."

The next day I walked in and sat down. Vernon was cutting a young man's hair and talking with another gentleman. Another barber was cutting hair in the third chair. I flipped through a magazine and waited.

"I can get you next," Mr. Winfrey said.

In a few moments the clippers were going, and we were engaged in pleasant conversation. I noticed an old newspaper on the wall with a huge headline that read:

Vernon Winfrey–# 1 Barber in Tennessee.

I asked:

"Were you really the best barber in Tennessee?"

He chuckled. Then I noticed the masthead of the newspaper. It read:

"Hillbilly News."

"A friend brought me that from Gatlinburg," he said.

Several people came in: a former Nashville city council

member, a preacher who works with drug addicts, a current city council member, a lawyer, and a retired Fisk University professor. I quietly enjoyed their conversation so much I didn't even notice the time.

Mr. Winfrey spent about an hour on my haircut. Toward the end he whispered:

"When I first moved my shop here, this was a white neighborhood. I had one white man who started coming to me and I cut his hair for many years, even after the neighborhood changed."

I was pleased with my haircut and with the time and attention Mr. Winfrey devoted to me. I really enjoyed the people. And I couldn't have asked to be treated any better. It was a wonderful experience.

So why was I afraid to get a haircut with a college professor, city council members, a preacher, and a lawyer? Could it be that the "color line" still plagues us in Twenty-First-Century America?

I've had many, many experiences (like my haircut with Mr. Winfrey) where crossing the color line and going beyond race was a lot of fun. Hopefully this book will help you be a part of that fun. So, come along; unwind, be kind, and enjoy a nice blend of "tea" (community and diversity) with me!

5 Colorful People & A Drab, Gray Elephant in A Dark Room

I once heard a story about an elephant which can give us a lot of insight about racial perspectives. I changed the story a bit to make it more colorful.

Five people were recruited to help a researcher with a project: a white man; a brown man; a black woman; a red woman; and, a yellow man. The researcher said that he was going to send them all into a dark room together. Once they entered, they were to feel around until they found an object . . . then hold on to it until everybody found something. So, they did.

Then, while still in complete darkness, the researcher asked each person to describe what he or she was touching. The white man said it was a sword-like object with a sharp point. The brown man said he was holding on to a floppy piece of leather. The black woman said she was pushing against a wall. The red woman said she was holding a big brush with a long, bendable handle. Then the yellow man said he was holding on to the trunk of a tree.

At that point the researcher turned the lights on. The white man was holding the tip of a tusk. The brown man was holding on to a big ear. The black woman was pushing against a huge body. The red woman was holding a tail. And the yellow man had his arms wrapped around a leg.

They were all touching various parts of the same elephant in the room. I think that's what we do with race in America. We're all holding on to different perspectives of the very same elephant. Perhaps our individual and color-group perspectives are a bit narrow. Maybe we need to listen to diverse perspectives to get the full picture.

I love quotations, and, especially, "quotable" ones. They often turn on the light for me and give me a lot of insight and understanding which otherwise I wouldn't have. I've collected quotes for several decades and will race to share some of them with you in this book. (I also like puns.) Here are a few elephant quotes and the racial insights they give me:

> "Race in this country is still the elephant in the room, that nobody wants to discuss." – Lenny Kravitz –

Hey, Lenny, let's do something adventurous and step into the dark room of race in America. Let's set aside our defensive silence, break out of the mold of clichés, and discuss race in an open, honest, compassionate, and heart-felt way.

> "When you have got an elephant by the hind legs and he is trying to run away, it's best to let him run." – Abraham Lincoln –

Maybe we could let go of our negative views of people who are not the same color as we are?

> "Words are cheap. The biggest thing you can say is "elephant." – Charlie Chaplin –

Next time you are tempted to think you know the whole story about a racial situation; say "elephant" and remember this story.

> "I always think I look like Elephant Man – I can't get used to my own image." – Brian Cox –

We all have that problem, Brian, some of us just have trouble admitting it. And the misconstrued concept of race in America often makes it even harder to like your own image.

> "People are so difficult. Give me an elephant any day." --Mark Shand –

Sorry Mark, in America we all have to interact with people of all types. We can't just hang with elephants.

> "If you are neutral in situations of injustice, you have chosen the side of the oppressor. If an elephant has its foot on the tail of a mouse and you say that you are neutral, the mouse will not appreciate your neutrality." – Desmond Tutu –

I can't argue with that, Desmond.

> "I get an urge, like a pregnant elephant, to go away and give birth to a book." – Stephen Fry –

That's what I'm doing as I write this.

> "A lot of people are afraid of the idea of enslavement, and that's because it's tied to so much shame and guilt . . . That's the big elephant in the room, but a

part of why we're afraid to attack that subject matter is because of the way we've been taught about it." – Aldis Hodge –

Are you ready to learn some fresh, encouraging, and healing ways to think about race? Let's go for it!

So how can we move beyond America's racial pain? "One bite at a time." (However, it's much too great for one individual or color-group to deal with this topic alone; so perhaps we need to begin to *dine* together cross-culturally.)

The Treasure of Me and My Color

One goal of this book is to cultivate and release color-kindness in people of every skin complexion. Race and color are difficult to discuss. We live in a culture that has conditioned people of all colors to believe that color matters, for better or for worse, even when we want to say that it doesn't.

To truly value the various shades of humanity, we need to go beyond **color-apathy** and begin to experience and spread **color-appreciation**. However, until we truly accept and value our own color, it's almost impossible to accept and appreciate the various colors of others.

In one-on-one relationships it's easy to be colorblind and ignore a person's individual epidermis coloration, however, in broader society, there's really no way that we can ignore the fact that differences in skin pigmentation exist. We are surrounded with color diversity every day and it is easy to move into an uncomfortable *us vs. them* attitude. However, much of our uneasiness about skin color comes from fake news—from centuries of misinformation.

I think one thing that all my readers can agree on is this: Everybody deserves to be comfortable in her own skin. So, to help us start on a positive and encouraging footing, I wrote an uplifting affirmation called:

The Treasure of Me and My Color

An amazing treasure has been hidden on earth—unrecognized and undiscovered for centuries. This extraordinary treasure has been confused with the common and the ordinary. The treasure is me and my color.

I am a unique person who overcame unimaginable odds when I first appeared on this planet. Statistically my existence is impossible. But here I am. My very existence declares that I am a magnificent winner. I am an indescribable treasure—full of value. In fact, I am priceless.

My worth is infinite. All the good things I see around me—all the things that I or anybody else could ever own—are worth nothing when compared with my value and with the value of each person I meet.

From this point on in my life, I will no longer fail to

recognize and appreciate the **_treasure of me_**. I will take good care of the treasure of me and use it wisely. I will treat myself with all the kindness and respect due someone of unlimited value! I will avoid self-put-downs and self-destruction.

I will also treasure all the other infinitely valuable human beings on the planet and their color (whatever it may be). I will recognize and respect the treasure of them. I will see myself as a statistical miracle living on a planet of other human miracles. And I will celebrate my life and the life of other people of all complexions.

Because of my tremendous value, I will **_value life_**. At my conception there were 400 million sperm and only one could produce me; so, at that moment I overcame unbeatable odds. Now I am an incredible winner—an amazing odds beater—and I will beat any obstacle life may put in my way. I will continue to be a winner my entire life by recognizing and accepting my winning status as the treasure of me and the value of me and my color.

Nothing or no one can devalue me but myself and I refuse to do that. Problems, circumstances, other people's behaviors, put-downs, economics, even sickness or ultimately death—nothing can devalue me because the treasure of me and my color is much more than just a cosmic accident. As Mother Teresa of Calcutta saw infinite value in the poorest human being because of Christ, so I can always find value in me and in the billions of other people in our colorful human race.

Nothing can devalue me . . . I choose not to devalue myself or others. I feel good! I celebrate! I love people! I serve. I honor and respect people of all colors. I am part of the most important enterprise in the universe: multicolored-multicultural human life! We are all made in the image of our Creator.

What am I worth? I can never describe or define my value. So, instead, I will experience it. I will believe in it. I will treasure it. I will live it. I will share my sense of value with people of all colors.

What an honor I have to be alive. I am grateful for the ***treasure of me*** and my color.

Cross-Color Builders Experience the Treasure of Color

In 2002 Coretta Scott King said:

> "We're a long way from realizing the dream. We need to bring people together across racial, religious, and cultural lines. Then our biases will disappear. And we can make that happen."

In America today, the chasm between whites and blacks is painfully obvious, especially on the political front. We need to build bridges beyond the colors, experiences, and beliefs that divide us.

Horace King, a slave, was a real bridge builder. He was born in 1807 in South Carolina with a mixed ethnic heritage of African American, Native American, and white. His second owner, John Godwin, was a covered bridge builder. In the 1830s Godwin moved from South Carolina to west Georgia and took King with him. Although Horace King was legally Godwin's *property* according to American law, actually, King acted more as Godwin's junior partner.

Together they built the first bridge across the Chattahoochee River (a 560 feet long covered bridge) between Columbus, Georgia and Phenix City, Alabama. A few years later a major flood washed the bridge down the river; Godwin and King were hired to rebuild it. Historians give King credit for making the second bridge successful because he was able to salvage pieces of the old bridge and successfully meet the deadline for the new one.

In 1846 Godwin gave King his legal freedom; the Alabama state legislature passed a bill making King's freedom official. When Godwin died in 1849, King spent $1,000 (a huge amount in those days) to place a beautiful headstone over Godwin's grave in Phenix City. He inscribed on the headstone: "This stone was placed here by Horace King in lasting remembrance of the love and gratitude he felt for his friend and former master."

After Godwin's death, King moved around the South as a free man and an independent contractor. He built covered bridges in Georgia, Tennessee, Alabama, and Mississippi. He also built homes, commercial buildings, and a self-supported wooden staircase that is still one of the most amazing features of the Alabama State Capitol Building. One of Horace Kings' covered bridges remains in use today in Meriwether County, Georgia, southwest of Atlanta.

After the Civil War, King served four years in the Alabama State Legislature before moving to LaGrange, Georgia in the 1870s. There he continued building and brought his sons into his construction business. When Horace King died, business stopped in LaGrange while both blacks and whites came to pay their respects as his funeral procession moved through the streets.

Horace King can serve as a powerful example for us in the Twenty-first Century. Although he was a victim of slavery, he chose to see beyond hatred and blame and do what he could to build bridges. He found a way to cross over his pain into an amazing life. If we will emulate the pattern set by King and **build relationship bridges**, we can replace racial friction with the healing power of color kindness.

However, like King and Godwin, we have to work together as friends. Together we can build a bridge from Columbus to Phenix City. Columbus represents America's painful history of conquest, dominance, and slavery. Phenix City represents healing, new life, and genuine brotherhood.

Just as a flood wiped out King's and Godwin's first bridge, we, too, may have to sometimes rebuild bridges when they are washed away. Too many people give up on cross-color relationships if their first bridge fails. But like King, salvage what you can and rebuild. Then reach out and begin building cross-color bridges everywhere. We also need to teach our sons and daughters to build bridges like Horace King did.

It's time for us to move beyond race in the 21st century! If in the middle of active slavery, King and Godwin could have such amazing trust, friendship, and love for one another, surely, we can as well. Are you a Columbus to Phenix City bridge builder?

Hop Along With Me

I don't like frog legs. I won't eat frog legs. I find frog legs totally disgusting. But the truth is, I've never given frog meat a chance.

I am so terribly offended with the idea of eating a slimy green wart-maker's legs, that I just can't put those lily pad jumpers in my mouth. (Oh, once or twice I have forced a nibble, but I think my taste buds were petrified. Anyway, I already knew I didn't like it.)

The taste somehow doesn't seem very important to me. Frog legs may taste like chicken, but I can't taste the chicken for the toad.

I just don't like frog legs! Okay. And I don't like being pressured to give them a sincere try. I don't like them because I don't want to like them.

I guess I might be a little prejudiced.

"A little prejudiced!" you say.

Well, okay. I admit it. When you talk about eating toad toes, I'm jumping to conclusions. I'm like the guy who said:

"I've got my mind made up, don't confuse me with the facts."

When it comes to eating croaker crutches, I'm the guy who is so narrow-minded that he can see through a key hole with both eyes at the same time.

Do you see my problem? I am so offended by frogs (I don't even like tadpoles), that's why I refuse to give frog meat an honest try. I don't know why I am so prejudiced against frog legs. However, if I thought that my not eating frog legs was hurting people, I would make myself change. Prejudice is strong, but I could overcome it, if I really wanted to.

In the world today, however, there is a far more dangerous prejudice that we need to avoid and overcome. Prejudice against people's skin color still exists. We still classify people by "race."

However, people are just people. There is not "an us and a them." There is just "a me and a you." And you and I can get along if we get to know each other as individual people instead of as human categories.

Am I Out Of Step With Truth?

Yes, I am. To varying degrees (like the colorful people with the elephant) we all are out of step with the whole truth. Like me with the frog legs—we sometimes let our emotions and desires influence our beliefs and our actions. So, as you read this book, anywhere you see me out of step, know that it isn't intentional or unkind. I'm doing my best to understand race beyond my *white* perspective, so I strive to be correctable and willing to change. I'm open to your feedback. I am sincerely seeking truth and fresh perspectives that lead to healing and solving America's racial divide; especially, between blacks and whites.

Actually, I've been out of step a lot in my life. I've preached in several black churches and I've been on the platform with the ministers in many of them. Often there is a well-rehearsed choir behind the ministers; also, when they sing, the ministers and the congregation all stand up clapping and swaying along with the choir. So, I would attempt to sway and clap with them. However, I always felt out of step and my wife would later confirm to me that indeed I was. When the choir swayed one way, I swayed the other. When the choir clapped on one beat, I clapped on the other. I can't imagine what I'd be doing with a group of hula dancers in Hawaii.

Once, however, I felt completely in the groove, right in sync with my brothers and sisters in Christ. I believed that I had finally learned to flow in step with the music.

After the service, I went up to my wife, Ernie, and said, "It's a miracle! I was finally in rhythm with the choir." She looked me in the eye and said, "The miracle is that you thought you were!"

What Color Is A Human Kidney?

Under the skin all people have the same anatomy. It's human anatomy, not black, white, red, brown, or yellow anatomy!

Inside all people there is a rainbow of color diversity. Your 78 organs and 13 organ systems are various colors and shades. However, fortunately for you, they all get along with each other and work together (without color prejudice) to keep you alive. Color diversity is no threat to your organs.

People of various skin colors have the exact same color bouquet of organ colors. If only we could see inside each other, our inner color scheme would be the same. (Too bad we humans don't have transparent skin.)

Human kidneys and gallbladders are reddish brown, the same color as a kidney bean. If you have them, you're partially a red man or red woman on the inside, no matter what your outside color.

Human spleens are brown. So, at least on the inside, you're partly a brown person.

Human bones are white. Therefore, regardless of your skin color, you are somewhat of a white person on the inside.

Human gallbladders are green. Therefore, you are part green on the inside. (Does that make you part Martian?)

Aren't you glad that the various colors inside your body work together in peace and harmony? Aren't you glad that your organs aren't segregated and refusing to cooperate with each other or even refusing to live in the same body together? I sure am!

Perhaps we need to look at everybody we meet "under the skin." Here's a short poem I wrote about that:

> Under the skin we're all the same colors;
> Organs, brains, bones, and blood.
> Under the skin we think and we pray
> And live day by day,
> Doing our best to find our way.
> Under the skin we hope and dream
> And envision a better world
> And a better life for us and others.
> So isn't it time that we look within
> And see the unity of all people under the skin?

Race Forward

2. From Colorblind to Color Appreciation

Saying Fresh Things in New Ways

I love to write and try to say things in a way that no one has ever said before. Here are some of my attempts to be original in my thinking about race and color:

> *Humanity is like a box of colored pencils. When we appreciate our various colors, we can draw beautiful images together.*
>
> *Variety of skin color is everywhere you look. That is one of the most visible human characteristics. Life is less stressful if you view varieties of skin color as an asset rather than as a threat.*
>
> *Skin shade doesn't identify different races. Instead, it adds colorful variety to the human race. Unfortunately, appreciating skin color is an art that many people never take the time to acquire.*
>
> *No law can make people appreciate and enjoy color diversity. That takes an eye for illumination and a heart of love.*
>
> *Skin-color-appreciation is not created by passivity. It requires active, caring interaction, and insightful understanding.*

My Story

I grew up in Arkansas and Tennessee, colorblind and naive to the racial discrimination all around me. Although I've always had a deep sense of right and wrong, when I was growing up I hardly noticed racial injustice. I was pretty much unaware of the many ways African Americans who lived around me were being mistreated.

One of my earliest memories is going to downtown Little Rock with my mother and asking her why there were two water fountains. She told me that one was for white people and the other was for **colored** people. I asked why, and she said that she didn't know. (Without honest history, none of us know the real reasons that was done.) Even as a four-year-old, it seemed wrong to me to make people drink out of a water fountain that matched their skin color.

Although growing up in the South, I was seldom around (and rarely even saw) black people. My early schools I attended were all white. However, my parents did hire a black woman a few times to help them around our house. I was so unaware of race that she was like a novelty to me. Really, unless I asked a question, the subject of race never came up in my home. Also, at that time, it was very rare to see blacks on TV.

However, there was a major racial incident in Little Rock the year I started the first grade there. Members of the Army's 101st Airborne Division were sent to our city to integrate Central High

School. At the time I was so colorblind that I didn't really understand what was going on and why the army needed to be in our town to help some teenagers go to school.

I remember the American troops weren't fondly spoken of for being in 1957 Arkansas like they were for being in Iraq and Afghanistan. I don't remember seeing or hearing about any "We Support Our Troops" signs back then.

At that time, I lived at 3724 West 21st Street and was in the first grade at Garland (*Whites Only*) Elementary School. My father's job put him somewhat in the middle of the integration conflict. He worked for a Little Rock radio station and did news reports from Central High School during the turmoil.

Central High School was successfully integrated by the Little Rock Nine (9 innocent teenagers) and the Army. However, today, the Little Rock school district is predominantly black.

My parents were passively colorblind. I don't think they agreed with segregation, but they never said or did anything against it. And although I was living in the middle of it, segregation was so effective, I hardly knew black people existed. I had an uncle who I would see a few times a year who was an outspoken racist. He would use racial slurs in our home. I didn't like to hear them. Eventually I began to speak out against his racial remarks. When he would make verbal insults about black people (even though there were none around in our home), then I would speak up:

"What about those white people?"

He would just look at me and ignore me.

I went to elementary school in Arkansas and was taught a course on Arkansas history. Slavery was presented as kind and paternal. The slaveholders were caring for their slaves who were too backward to take care of themselves. So, they took them in like family. Because the slaves were valuable possessions, the "owners" always treated them well. The slaves were happy in their work and sang a lot.

My memory is that the text books contained iconic pictures of Antebellum plantation mansions with slaves happily serving their "masters" and even providing loving childcare for them. It showed slaves in the fields, happily toiling away. It had pictures of tribal Africans and implied that the slaves were far better off than they would have been if they were left in Africa. The slaveholders had "civilized" them, while creating a great Antebellum culture for them in which they could participate.

I never went to school with black people until I was in the tenth grade. By then my family was living in Jackson, Tennessee. My high school had about 1,000 students and only a tiny token of that number was black. They were easily lost in the crowd. I don't recall ever having the slightest interaction with any of them. I don't even remember a black person being in any of my high school classes.

During my high school years, the Civil Rights Movement was going strong; but I was so colorblind to race and racism, I never even knew exactly about what people were protesting. Martin Luther King, Jr. was murdered when I was in the 11th grade; this saddened me greatly. However, at that time in my life, I really didn't know for what he stood.

As hard as it is to imagine, I had no idea blacks were being mistreated because of their skin color. I didn't know they could not vote in the South. It didn't dawn on me blacks were forced to stay in their own neighborhoods. I didn't know violence was used against them if they tried to break out of the status quo. I lived through the Civil Rights Movement in a white, live-and-let-live, colorblind cloud.

Here's an odd thing about my high school. There was an all-black high school directly across the street from my high school. Yet, believe it or not, it never even registered in my mind there was something wrong with that. I never went on that campus and never thought about the irony of another high school being across the street from mine. Two years after I graduated, the city built a pedestrian walkway over the busy street between the schools and combined them into one high school.

After graduating, I went to college and I still had no interaction with and hardly any awareness of black people. Of course, by then Motown Music was popular, so I did hear a lot of that. I wasn't intentionally trying to avoid blacks. There were just hardly any around me.

During my freshman year in college I was recruited to sell books (dictionaries) door-to-door for my summer job. I was sent to Austin, Texas. It was quite a learning experience. It was the first time in my life that I interacted with different races. I spent 12 1/2 hours a day knocking on doors in white, black, and Hispanic neighborhoods and my colorblindness began to melt. I noticed a big difference in how I was treated in different neighborhoods.

To my surprise, most white people weren't very friendly to solicitors. In white neighborhoods, I was frequently spoken to rudely, sometimes told to get off their porches, had doors slammed on me, and even had a gun pulled on me once. It was terribly discouraging.

However, in black and Hispanic neighborhoods, people were very friendly. When I knocked on their screen door, people would often yell from within the house: "Come on in." So, I would. (Many homes still weren't airconditioned.) They would often offer me something to drink and sometimes something to eat. People very respectively listened to my book presentation and were often very ready to buy my books. (Even when they didn't buy, they were nice about it.) By the end of the summer, I realized that I really liked blacks and Hispanics.

Afterwards I went back to college and met a guy from India. We became great friends and he taught me a lot about his culture. He was a Hindu and I was a Christian, so we talked a lot about the differences in our beliefs, but neither of us saw those differences as a threat. He went home with me often and became a great friend of my entire family. However, I still must have been somewhat colorblind because I still hardly noticed, nor did I interact with the few blacks on my campus.

I was recruited to sell books for a second summer. However, this time I was asked to sell a three-volume set of books called *Ebony's Pictorial History of Black America*. I was sent to two towns across a river from each other; Columbus, Georgia, and Phenix City, Alabama. (The place where Horace King and John Goodwin built the bridge I told you about earlier.)

My sales territory was all black neighborhoods. It was the summer of 1971 and there were ongoing race riots in both towns. Also, the Black Panther Party was strong in the area—I even sold books to several of them! The Black Panthers were always very nice to me.

As I began to knock on doors to sell black history books that summer, I was once again, very well received. I wrote this about that summer:

> You don't shoot salesmen, do you?" asked a 20-year-old white boy as he stood on a black man's front porch in Columbus, Georgia during the racial uprising of the summer of 1971. The smiling white boy was wearing a T-shirt, shorts, and sandals; and holding a sample copy of *Ebony's Pictorial History of Black America*.

"Oh no! No Sir! We don't shoot salesmen. Come on in here." said the black man. The white boy warmly shook the black man's hand as he walked into the living room and asked, "May I sit down?"

"Have a seat." the black man said and pointed to a couch covered with clear plastic. Above the couch was a picture of three men; Martin Luther King, Jr, President Kennedy, and Bobby Kennedy. Beside that was a picture of a black Jesus.

The white boy sat down and began to flip through the pages of his *Ebony* sample book. He showed pictures of slavery, lynching, segregation, police dogs, Madame C. J. Walker, Jackie Robinson, and even the Jackson Five.

Somewhere during the sales presentation, however, the white boy asked the black man if he knew Jesus as his Savior. The black man smiled from ear-to-ear and said; "I couldn't have made it without Jesus!"

"The white boy said: "I love Him too!" He put down the sample book and they began to talk excitedly about "sweet Jesus." Before long they were holding hands and praying for each other. Then they embraced warmly, both wiping away tears. When the white boy left, the black man said, "You be careful, Son!"

The white boy said, "Thank you, brother. You too!" Then he walked across the yard to the small house next door. He knocked on the door. A black lady opened the door. The white boy said: "Hi, I'm Steve Simms. You don't shoot salesmen, do you?"

This happened many times a day that summer as I sold black history books door-to-door in the middle of a racial uprising in Columbus, Georgia. A few times I went into my "territory" and found a white-owned grocery store had been burned out. Once I was knocking on doors when police in riot gear marched down the street. But I was never threatened, never harmed, and almost always was warmly received.

Many times, I would be showing my book only to find out my prospect was a Christian. I would lay the book down to have wonderful interaction with my Christian brother or sister. We would share our personal experiences about God's work in our lives and pray for each other, sometimes for hours. I was always amazed at the intimacy and love we different-colored "strangers" felt for each other.

I vividly remember one day when I was feeling discouraged and homesick. Suddenly a large black woman came around the corner of her house right in front of me. She was singing, *Where Could I Go But To The Lord?*

I told her I was really discouraged and needed God's help. She put her hands on me and began to pray over me. It was one of those kinds of prayer that you can feel all over your body and way down into your soul.

I get excited thinking about it, even now, many years later. God is good! He's "better felt than *telt.*" I love how God wants to bless you and me through brothers and sisters of a different race.

While selling black history books, I started visiting black churches on Sundays, often by myself. I was always warmly accepted and treated very well. I was usually asked to stand up and say something in the meeting. I loved the passion and enthusiasm for Christ I saw in most of the black churches I attended.

That was quite a summer. The next year I sold Ebony's black history books again, this time in Greensboro and Burlington, North Carolina. I was so immersed in and accepted in black culture that if I ever saw a white person in the neighborhood, I would wonder what they were doing there.

Alternative View Of Color

One black church I visited by myself that summer gave me a different perspective on race. The preacher's sermon theme was:

"God created man and then He added color to His creation to beautify it."

He said:

"Everybody knows an unpainted house isn't very beautiful but needs color."

He boldly and enthusiastically gave many

advantages to having color.

As the only white person in the meeting, I began to feel somewhat self-conscious about my lack of color. I literally began to sink down in my seat (as if that would hide my white face).

After the sermon, while still in the pulpit, the preacher looked at me; warmly welcomed me; and asked if I would like to say something to the congregation. (I felt like an unpainted house.) I timidly stood up and said something like:

"I'm glad to be here. I love Jesus and He loves us no matter what color we are; whether we are painted or unpainted."

Then I sat down.

After the meeting people hugged me and greeted me as if nothing about inferiority because of racial differences had been said or implied. I had been put in a very uncomfortable situation, but everybody seemed unaware, colorblind as to how that made me feel.

It was eye-opening to have been on the other side of the racial divide—to be a minority in a group (the only white person) and to have my skin color publicly looked down on and criticized by someone representing the majority. It was also somewhat painful.

Afterwards, I thought a lot about that experience. If just a very few minutes of hearing my skin color mildly and politely demeaned by someone of another race, made me feel bad about myself, what has centuries of American racism done to African-Americans? I learned that it doesn't take mean-spirited, blatant name-calling, nor abuse to make people feel bad. Even brief mild statements of someone's supposed racial superiority, expressed in a friendly way, can hurt.

So, multiply my very momentary experience of being on the receiving end of mild racial disrespect, by living in a society that was built on hostile racial views toward dark skin color (infinitely worse than the preacher's unpainted house analogy) 24/7/365. I cannot even comprehend that degree of psychological pain!

I shared this story with a black friend of mine about my age. He said while growing up, he was called racial slurs almost every day. He would walk to school while white teenagers drove by calling him racist insults and throwing trash and other things at him.

More About My Struggles with My Own Colorblindness

After I graduated from college I went to a small seminary in Memphis, Tennessee. Although there were fewer than 150 students, it was the only truly racially mixed school I ever attended. Several of my classmates were black pastors.

Some of them belonged to a Memphis-based denomination, called the Church of God In Christ (COGIC for short). It is the second largest African-

American denomination in the United States. While I was attending seminary, it came to mind numerous times: Perhaps I should approach the COGIC leadership and see if I could become a pastor in their denomination.

I thought as a white-guy leading a congregation in a black denomination, I could attract both blacks and whites and help bring about some racial reconciliation. It was a nice thought, but I never acted on it (until many years later). Instead, I took the easier route of being ordained in my white, childhood denomination.

As a white pastor in a white denomination, I tried to reach out to blacks. I brought in black preachers and black Gospel singers for special events. The events would go well, but nothing would happen afterwards. The churches I led stayed all white. I would knock on doors in black neighborhoods (I had gotten good at that while selling black history books). I invited blacks to attend my white church, but they never did. (The unfairness of that never dawned on me at the time. I never thought that perhaps I should go to their church instead.)

Cross-Walking In Paducah, Kentucky

Once when I was an assistant pastor of a white church in Paducah, Kentucky, I began to pull an 8-foot cross with a bicycle training-wheel attached, around town. The local TV station and the local newspaper both did stories about me and the cross.

Soon after the publicity, I received a phone call. A man said that he was the president of the Paducah

Black Preachers' Association and asked if I would carry the cross to lead their city-wide, unity-day march. I said *yes* and was honored to have that opportunity.

When I arrived for the march, I was the only white person there. (I hadn't been able to get any friends or church members to go with me.) The leaders of the march put me about five feet in front of a long line of about 200 people, gave me the route, and asked me to lead the way. So, I started off and they followed.

Soon a young black man caught up with me and began to silently and awkwardly walk beside me. I said *hello*, but he didn't respond. After a few minutes, he looked at me and said:

"Is that the Lord's cross or the KKK?"

I quickly replied:

"The Lord's cross!"

We began to talk about race and about how sad it is that such a question would even need to be asked. We were both disturbed that the Lord's cross had been used as a symbol of white-supremacy, hatred, control, fear, injustice, and violence against innocent human beings.

After several minutes, my new friend turned to me and asked me:

"Can I carry the Lord's cross?"

While writing this memory just now, I began to weep and sob. There is still so much racial healing that needs to be done.

I took the cross off my shoulder and put it on his. And what had been used as a symbol of hate, became what God intended it to be, a symbol of love. Soon, other people came up beside us and took turns carrying the Lord's cross.

COGIC

After about 15 years, I gave up on being a preacher and became a full-time motivational speaker. It was so much easier than having to deal with and trying to overcome tradition, history, and religious control.

I got married to a woman named Ernie. My wife and I both pursued business. (She was a corporate trainer and facilitator.) However, she kept telling me that there was more that I should do than to be a motivational speaker. As a speaker, I spoke for more than half of the "municipal leagues" (the associations of mayors and city officials in each US state). In most states there were only a few black mayors and/or city officials. However, in the Southern states there were many. When I spoke for the Mississippi Municipal League Convention, more than half of the delegates were black. I loved seeing that one of the historically racist states in America had so many black mayors and city officials!

During that time Ernie had a dream. She dreamed that I was passionately preaching in a black church and that I was surrounded by fire. As I was thinking about her dream, I remembered the thought that kept coming to me in seminary, that I should approach the Church of God In Christ about becoming a pastor in their denomination.

Suddenly, this thought came across my mind: "You never acted on that leading." I felt so convicted that I immediately picked up the Nashville Yellow Pages and called every COGIC church in town. However, except for a few answering machines, no one answered.

To the answering machines I said something like, "Hello, I am a white minister and feel like God wants me to become part of the Church of God In Christ. Can you help me?" No one returned my call.

A few days later I called the COGIC headquarters in Memphis and someone gave me the home phone number of Pastor Larry Britton. I called him, and he invited me to come to a prayer meeting at the church he pastored. So, I went and afterwards I began to tell Pastor Britton about what God was doing in my heart. He encouraged me and invited me to visit again on a Sunday morning.

Soon after that, he invited me to preach at his church on a Sunday. It was my first time to preach in a black church—it was a wonderful experience. Then he asked if I would like to meet his bishop, Bishop James Scott. We had a phone conversation with the bishop and he asked me to come to Chattanooga to preach at his church. Then he scheduled me to come back in two weeks and talk to his official board.

Two weeks later I was sitting alone in a COGIC bishop's office waiting to be called into a board meeting. I kept thinking how amazing it was that I was there. Then they called me into their meeting.

There were about ten black preachers seated around a conference table. Most of them were older men. Bishop Scott told me to tell the board what I had told him. So, I told them about my wife's recent dream of me preaching in a black church and about my desire in seminary to pursue becoming a minister in the COGIC—but I never acted on that urge. I told them that I wanted to start a multi-racial church near my home.

After I finished, one of the men immediately said:

"If God sent him, we want him. I move we receive him."

Someone else said, "Second."

The Bishop took a vote—it was unanimous. Before I knew it, they were all hugging me and welcoming me into the Church of God In Christ; fully ordained and with equal standing as the other pastors.

After we sat down, one of the men looked at me and said:

"You do, by the way, believe our doctrine?"

I was happy to say "yes" to that. A little later that day the bishop brought me into a meeting of about

40 pastors that he led. The bishop introduced me to them and then told them how they had received me as a pastor and had commissioned me to start a multi-racial church in Franklin, Tennessee, just outside of Nashville. Suddenly they all stood up and gave me a standing ovation. Then it seemed like everybody in that room hugged me and welcomed me. These weren't cool, official hugs, but warm, enthusiastic, and personable. They gave me the warmest reception I have ever had from any group of people in my life.

They had a monthly ministers' meeting in Chattanooga, Tennessee, that I started attending and soon they asked me to teach a church history class every month. I loved riding to the meeting with some of my fellow Nashville pastors and interacting with about 40 African-American pastors every month. It was always an amazing time.

My wife, Ernie and I also went to quarterly Jurisdictional Meetings in Shelbyville, Tennessee, and other cities, every three months. At those meetings, a couple of hundred people would gather from about 15 churches and have a joint meeting. We were usually the only white people present. When I think back, I'm still amazed at how well we were received and embraced as equals.

White Guy on The Streets in The Hood

During that time, Ernie and I started a church (as COGIC pastors) in a small, historic black neighborhood (called Natchez) in Franklin—a very affluent city just south of Nashville. (The Natchez neighborhood is built right in the middle of the Civil

War battlefield where the Battle of Franklin took place and some of the streets are named for Confederate generals who died there. The name *Natchez* is also the name of the *Natchez Trace* which was a major human trafficking route for marching chain-gangs of enslaved people to the Deep South to be sold into brutal cotton field slavery. It seems ironic that for many years it was one of the segregated parts of Franklin where blacks were forced to live.)

We had no salary, but God provided just enough money to rent an old, rundown building that had been a notorious black night club called *The Big Wheel*. (People told us that the police used to be called there all the time.) One of the first people who started coming to the church, said on her first Sunday:

"I used to party in here and now I'm gonna party for the Lord!"

I began to regularly walk the streets of Natchez and talk to people. There was a parking lot where several men would hang out, often drinking and drugging. I started hanging out with them and talking with them. They began to tell me about their situations and allow me to pray over them. We became friends. They had unusual nick names like; Chicken Dinner, Peter Pan, Fuzzy, Buster, Little Bear, Big Bear, and then some normal names like Bill and Rashid.

I used to regularly go to all the houses and apartments in the neighborhood and talk to people.

I was used to that from my time selling black history books. However, the first time Ernie went with me, she was a little nervous. I parked the car, but she said that didn't seem like a safe place to leave the car; so, I drove to another place. Then she said the same thing about that place; therefore, I said something like:

"We're about to be walking these streets so if it is safe enough for us, it should be safe for the car."

As we started knocking on doors together, we had a funny moment. A guy opened his door and shook both our hands. Then he said:

"I've been cleaning chitlins (pig intestines), I guess I should have let you know."

I am a bit of a germ freak, so I reacted by making noises and wiping my hand on my pants. Ernie began to laugh and told the gentleman how I was "scared of germs" and then he began to laugh, too. Soon all three of us were having a wonderful time laughing and talking together. After that, Ernie had no fear of knocking on doors in black neighborhoods anymore.

Although our Sunday morning meetings were small, they were wonderful in spirit and diversity. Instead of me being the authority and lecturing everybody, we met like family and allowed anyone present to speak in the meeting. As a multiracial group of equals we ministered to one another and prayed over each other like a loving support group.

From Colorblind to Color Appreciation

One day my mother asked me if she could prepare lunch one weekday each month and serve it to whomever wants to come from the community. So, we turned "The Big Wheel" into a lunch room. The guys from the parking lot, people from Sunday morning, and others from the neighborhood would gather to eat along with my mother and father. Then we would hang out together and enjoy each other's company. Those were wonderful lunches. Sometimes one of the guys would get up and tell a funny story or jokes or my dad would think of a few.

Ernie was in a Bible study at a big white church in the area, and women were hearing stories about what we were doing. A small group of women asked if they could also start cooking, and they started bar-b-queuing on the street right outside the former nightclub. It drew in everyone who could smell the smoke. Then they wanted to start doing activities in the small local park and invite the kids. They brought their own kids and served food and played games. These women got so excited they talked about it for years.

We eventually even started a food and clothing pantry to help the people in the community. After about 3 years of getting to know and be friends with many people in that neighborhood, we ran out of money to keep the building open and had to close it down.

Ernie's Surprise Experience of Discrimination

While we were reaching out to the Natchez community, Ernie and I were both part of several racial reconciliation groups in and around Nashville. Once Ernie and about six African-American, professional women decided to host and lead a women's conference. They planned it, organized it, and put a deposit on a meeting room in a large, nice, Brentwood, Tennessee hotel.

However, not as many people showed up at the conference as the leaders had anticipated. So, they went to the hotel staff and paid more than half the bill, explaining that because of the lower attendance it would take them a few days to pay the rest. Immediately after that, while the ladies who led the conference were still in the hotel meeting to discuss how the conference went and how to finish making the payment, a sales associate walked into the room and demanded payment in full.

They explained they had paid more than half the bill, but because of lower attendance they couldn't pay the rest for a few days. The sales associate ignored them and continued to demand immediate payment. Finally, the sales associate threatened to call the police. One of the ladies said:

"We are all tax paying citizens and will get this bill paid."

Ernie asked the sales associate:

"Will we have to get a lawyer for you to let us go?"

The hotel finally let the ladies go and they were able to pay the rest of the bill in a couple of days.

Ernie was shocked. She had never been treated like that before when dealing with a hotel. Suddenly she realized that she was the only white woman in the group. Later she told me:

"They would have never treated us that way had we been a group of white, professional women."

Later, Ernie asked one of the black women:

"How do you work your way through being treated like that?"

She answered:

"We have to because things like that happen to us every day."

The Salvation Army

As the Natchez ministry was winding down, Ernie saw an ad for a part-time job as a counselor with The Salvation Army. She sent in her resume. Soon she received a phone call about the job from someone who apparently thought she was a man. When they realized she was a woman they began to tell her that she would be counseling 86 men at night and would be the only staff person in the building. The HR person also told her she would be walking out into one of the most dangerous streets in downtown Nashville at ten o'clock at night.

Ernie asked them to hold on, got me, and told me to take the call; telling me this might be a good job for me. They invited me to come in for an interview and the next day I was hired to work for The Salvation Army Adult Rehabilitation Center in Nashville . . . an 86-bed alcohol and drug rehab. Usually, about 39% of the men were black, about 59% were white, and about 2% were other shades.

I had no idea I would be working with a total of about 1,400 men over the next 5 1/2 years nor how my heart would be so deeply touched. I loved those men and they loved me.

Our program was free, so men who came into the center had "hit bottom." They were broken, defeated, and humbled.

Part of my job was to interview every new man. They could sense I loved them—they trusted me; they told me their life stories in vivid detail. Black or white, each of the about 1,400 stories were different, but amazingly similar.

My heart broke for them. These guys had done everything conceivable to destroy their lives. They told me how they had lied, cheated, been negative, been abusive, freely engaged in every imaginable sexual activity, partied hard, been violent, shot people, abandoned their children, used every drug imaginable, been cruel to their wives and/or baby's mommas, stolen, and so much more.

They told me about the results of their "fun-seeking" behaviors. They had been overcome by anger, bitterness, and depression. They lost relationships with some (if not all) of the most important people in their lives. They lost job after job. They had lost any sense of self-worth. Many had been homeless. Many had been to jail and/or prison. Many had court orders against them. They were controlled by their cravings; their desires had defeated them.

Many wept. I cried with them. Most of them stayed in the program for a few days to a few months and then went back to their same self-destruction. Some came through several times.

While I was there I knew 17 of the guys who died in their self-destruction. I spoke at a few of their funerals. However, some of the guys did turn around and are clean and sober to this day.

I recognized each man's color; they were not blind to each other's color. However, in my 5 ½ years working there, I never heard (or heard of) a single racial put-down; and I never heard (or heard of) a racially motivated argument or fight. It was an amazing example of love and genuine reconciliation that went **beyond race.**

It's been several years since I worked there. Occasionally, I will see guys from there. They come up and hug me and thank me for working with them.

Bob's Racial Trauma

One man who finished the 6-month program and became a resident supervisor employed by the center, I'll call "Bob" to protect his identity. Bob was a black man, a few years older than I. He told me two stories about his racial experiences that deeply grieved me.

Once when Bob was homeless, he was sleeping in some woods just outside of a clearing. In the middle of the night he suddenly heard a lot of noise that woke him up. He looked in the direction of the noise and saw a bunch of white men, dragging a black man into the clearing from the other side. Bob watched as they put a noose around the man's neck and lynched him from a tree in the center of the clearing. He knew if he made any sounds they would probably find him and murder him as well. So, he was silent. (More than 4,000 documented lynchings of blacks by whites took place between 1880 and 1960.)

After the man was dead, they cut him down. Then they took a knife and began to mutilate his body. After their gory cruelty, they left laughing and drinking. Bob was afraid to move for hours. The next morning, he got as far away from that community as possible.

Another time, Bob was walking down a road when a pickup truck stopped. There were 4 or 5 white guys riding in the back, sitting on an old mattress. They asked Bob if he would like a ride. He said that he would and got into the back with the other men. Then the truck started down the road.

After having a casual conversation with him for a while, the men suddenly all jumped on Bob and began to beat him. He resisted but soon one of the men folded the mattress over on him as the others continued to beat him. The men got a rope and began to wrap it around the mattress and Bob. They pulled the rope tight. Then they lifted him up and rolled him and the mattress over the side of the moving truck, laughing as they did. Miraculously, Bob only suffered minor injuries.

Although what those guys in that truck did could have easily killed Bob (remember, he had seen white men murder a defenseless black man); yet, he had no color animosity. I don't know how Bob avoided racial hatred, but when I knew him, he was loving and kind to everybody. Even though he had encountered some cruel white people, Bob chose to go beyond race and never saw all white people as evil. Instead of judging me for my white skin color, he accepted me as a brother.

Salvation Army Inner City Community Center

A couple of years after I started working for the rehab center, Ernie was hired by The Salvation Army to run a multifaceted community center in a dangerous, predominantly black, Nashville neighborhood. There were shootings in the neighborhood at least twice a month. However, our experience in the Natchez neighborhood of Franklin had prepared her.

She oversaw numerous programs designed to help people in the community; she got to know many neighborhood people. She helped start a basketball league for a hundred young kids and recruited many volunteers to help with it. She led other programs which helped "human development."

We both felt like we needed to get out of the buildings in which we worked—desiring to get back onto the streets. So, Ernie, I and Linda (who worked there), and Ashish Pawar (a young man from India), along with others, began to *prayer walk* the neighborhood once a week. Sometimes the women who had helped us in Franklin would prepare sandwiches to give away.

We carried a full size, red, yellow, and blue, Salvation Army Flag with us which represented the blood of Jesus (red), the fire of the Holy Spirit (yellow), and a clean lifestyle (blue). Every time we hit the streets, we would meet various people (almost all black)—most of them wanted us to pray for them.

Once the police stopped us as we were about to walk down Second Street. They said:

"You don't want to go down there; it's the most dangerous drug street in Nashville."

Someone with us replied:

"We feel like we're supposed to go down that street, so we need to do it. Do you want to go with us?"

They said *no*—that meant we were on our own—then they drove away.

Tough looking African-American guys frequently stood on the curb on Second Street, sometimes holding up clear plastic bags full of white powder. Cars would occasionally pull up, make a quick transaction and move on.

They would ask us, "What's that flag?" We would answer their question. Many times, we would interrupt a drug deal where they would be stuffing the evidence in their pockets. However, no one ever got angry, mean, or violent with us. Those guys were hurting. They were trying to get by in life the only way they knew how. They were always kind to us.

Once when we were walking down Second Street, a tough looking man, standing with two rough looking women who looked like they might be prostitutes, demanded:

"What flag is that?"

I told him that it stood for the blood of Jesus and the fire of the Holy Spirit. His mouth fell open and he said:

"For you to bring that flag into this neighborhood, you gotta be from God."

Then he said:

"If I had grown up under a flag like that, my life would have been different!"

We asked his name and he said, "Chief." We began to have a great conversation with Chief and the two women. Soon someone asked if we could pray for them. They all said *yes*. So, we gathered around them and prayed. Afterwards, we were all wiping tears from our eyes, including Chief.

Another time we were carrying the flag down Second Street and a couple of guys began to talk to us. Soon several more walked over to us and joined in the conversation. Someone said:

"We'd like to pray for you guys."

They all began joining hands with us in a circle. As different ones of us took turns praying, more people came and joined in the circle. By the time we finished praying, there were ten or twelve people holding hands and praying together in the middle of the worst drug street in Nashville.

Starting A Salvation Army Church in The Hood

About five years after I started at the rehab center, The Salvation Army approached Ernie and me and asked if we would like to start a "nontraditional church" in that neighborhood. We told them we would love to do it. So, after several months of paperwork, on the first Sunday in March 2008, we started The Salvation Army Berry Street. A few years before that Ernie had heard these words in the middle of the night: "It would be next to impossible to start a church in downtown Nashville," and now here we were.

Although I love to preach (a "professional sermon"), we met more like a support group of equals, and let anybody present speak in the meeting as they felt led. In the beginning the meetings were probably about 80% black and 20% white. We also would invite a guest each week to come and share their story about how they came to know Christ.

We were surprised that when a white person would be our guest, he or she would usually start talking about having a black friend or having visited a black church. It seemed like our white guests felt like they had to show our mostly black congregation they weren't racist. However, when we had a black guest share, he or she never mentioned race. The black attendees were always gracious about that.

We also had anywhere from 25 to 35 black kids come from the neighborhood every Sunday. Almost all of them came on their own, without a parent. For 9 ½ years, various young adults, almost all of them white, would come every Sunday and lead a children's church program for the children. Those young adults were truly inspirational. They freely gave their time and love so faithfully to care for inner city children who were growing up in very difficult circumstances—so amazing!

One of them, Arash (of Iranian heritage) taught the children and teenagers faithfully for 7 ½ years. Several times Arash let black teenagers, who for various reasons were homeless, live in his home. He also hired them to work in his car dealership if they were willing. He's a guy who's incredible about showing color-appreciation. Also, we were able to have a snack for the kids every week.

Our adult meetings eventually grew to around 50-50 black and white. We usually would have between 25 and 35 adults who would open up their hearts to one another, encourage one another, and pray for one another on Sunday mornings. It was an incredible thing to see every week. We also had an Indian guy and sometimes some Hispanics.

Back to 1957 Again

When we first started Berry Street, I was browsing at a book store and saw a chapter in a book about how a few black first-graders integrated Glenn School in Nashville in 1957. I read about how Jacqueline Griffith, Lajuand Street, and Sinclair Lee Jr. walked through more than 200 white demonstrators on their first day of school, as one man yelled: "We've got to defy this thing!" Fortunately, the three children safely got into the school, but they were frequently harassed.

Those kids, like me, were born in 1951. I had a difficult time starting school. I couldn't imagine how hard it would have been if I were to have attended a different school with a different race of kids. I can't imagine how I would have felt on my first day of school if 200 adults of that race were yelling racist slurs at me. So, I decided to see if I could find one of those children; I did, I found one of the girls. I went to her home and listened to the details of her story.

I told her Ernie and I and a few other people would love to meet her on the anniversary of her first day of school at the exact time and spot where she went into the school because we wanted to apologize for the way she was treated. She humbly accepted the invitation and asked if she could bring her mother.

So, on that morning about 15 people, black and white, met in front of the Glenn School. Several of us white people present offered our sincere apologies, which she graciously received. Then we all joined hands in a circle and several people prayed for God's forgiveness and for the healing of the racial divisions in our country.

After that we walked a couple of blocks back to Berry Street and then watched a short documentary about the integration of the Glenn School. Then we had some refreshments and enjoyed each other's company for a while. It was a beautiful experience.

A Sad Ending to Our Multi-Racial Community

During our 9 ½ years at Berry Street, we were wonderfully supported and encouraged by our own Salvation Army leaders and by almost all The Salvation Army leaders who heard about Berry Street. However, eventually one formerly high ranking, retired leader (a white guy), thought we should meet like a traditional church. Although he was leading a "social justice center," he began to work behind the scenes to shut down what was happening. Eventually he was able to use his influence to bring a younger leader (another white guy) into Nashville, who felt the same way he did.

After his arrival, the new leader demanded we have a traditional sermon and stop letting people freely speak from their heart in the meeting. It was clear to us he didn't understand or appreciate all the years of individual transformation and relationship building which had occurred, or the breadth of it. So, after 9 ½ years of amazing racial reconciliation, unity and love, we felt we had no choice but to leave.

Although we are not sure what is coming next, we are excited about the upcoming chapter of our lives. We can't wait to connect with more colorful people of various shades. (If you would like to read more about what we did with The Salvation Army, search for my book: *Beyond Church: An Invitation To Experience The Lost Word Of The Bible—Ekklesia*.)

Here's one other experience we had while at Berry Street. The Salvation Army leaders in Murfreesboro, Tennessee were talking to Ernie and me about some people who were being disruptive on the property. I felt prompted to ask them if anything unusual had ever happened on The Salvation Army property prior to this time. They told me that a large tree stump on the property had been known as "the hanging tree." It was the place in town where blacks were lynched.

We asked them if we could bring some people to pray around the stump of that tree and ask God's forgiveness for the murders that were committed there by mobs of white people. They were excited for us to do that and wanted to be a part of it as well. So, a group of about twelve people gathered around the stump of the lynching tree and sincerely asked for God's forgiveness for the terrible evil done there. It's rather amazing, but afterwards, the people who were being disruptive changed their behavior. (You never know what negative connections there are in the spiritual realm, so it is good to repent for and clean up past personal and corporate sin.)

So Many Friends

Ernie and I through the years have made many black friends who we love and appreciate dearly. While I have been writing this, a young man has been staying in our home; consequently, he's been hearing a lot of these stories. The other day he said:

"You two are the only people I have ever heard talk about people in the hood like they're not from the hood."

Quoting him is making me cry. How is it that a 19-year-old white guy in Twenty-First Century America has never heard anyone talk about black people like they're equal to every other human being?

From Colorblind to Color Appreciation

3. My Top 10 Greatest Americans

American Greatness and The People Under the Skin!

Before we look more closely at race in America and examine the foundational history of black and white relationships, let's begin with the inspirational. There's a lot of greatness in American history. The leaders of the Civil Rights Movement frequently appealed to the greatness of our creeds. Martin Luther King, Jr. said:

> "I have a dream that one day this nation will rise up and live out the true meaning of its creed—we hold these truths to be self-evident that all men are created equal."

Here are my top 10 greatest Americans—the ten Americans who inspire me the most. I based this list on color-kindness—people who rose up to live out the true meaning of America's freedom creeds. How many of them have you heard about?

To me, these people courageously and heroically lived out the great American principle of *liberty and justice for all* more effectively than the rest of us Americans. Six of them were white and four were black. Four of them were women (two sisters share spot #6) and seven of them were men.

#10 – Dorothy Day

> "No one has a right to sit down and feel hopeless.

There is too much work to do." –Dorothy Day

"We believe in loving our brothers regardless of race, color or creed and we believe in showing this love by working for better conditions immediately." --Dorothy Day

Dorothy Day was born in 1897; she grew up in Chicago. She was very sensitive to the needs of others. As a young woman, she got involved with the communists. She abandoned traditional moral values, experimented with sexuality, and eventually had an abortion.

Later she met a man who was an atheist who wanted to escape from life. Dorothy moved to the beach and lived with him for three years, but she never could fully embrace his atheism. She got pregnant again; this time she refused to have an abortion. This broke up her relationship, so she moved to New York City with her new daughter.

There she met Peter Maurin, a French Catholic. Peter helped influence Dorothy to trust her heart's belief in God and to begin to obey God's leading.

Dorothy turned away from her old lifestyle and began to follow and obey Jesus. She said:

"My manifesto is the *Sermon on the Mount*."

In May 1933 she and Peter Maurin started a newspaper called *The Catholic Worker*. By 1936 it had more than 150,000 subscribers. Its goal was "to promote Catholic social teaching and to promote steps to bring about the peaceful transformation of society."

Homeless people began to come to her. She allowed several of them to live in her apartment with her and her daughter. Soon she began to start *Houses of Hospitality* to help feed and clothe and comfort the poor. Eventually, Dorothy took a vow of poverty to identify with all poor people. By 1936 she and Peter Maurin had opened 33 Catholic Worker *Houses of Hospitality* across the USA.

Dorothy Day felt the needs of others deeply—she was moved by the poverty and injustice around her. Throughout her life, she worked tirelessly to help people and to speak up for justice. She was arrested often in the struggle for civil rights, women's rights, worker's rights, and against war.

Dorothy's desire was to build a better world and to show the love of Jesus Christ to those who need Him the most. She said:

> "The greatest challenge of our day is: how to bring about a revolution of the heart, a revolution which has to start with each of us."

#9 - William Monroe Trotter

> "There can be no freedom without equality."— William Monroe Trotter

Standing almost alone during the Jim Crow days of forced segregation, open racism, and public lynchings in early Twentieth-Century America,

William Monroe Trotter boldly spoke out for equal rights. He was uncompromising in his stand for liberty and justice for all, targeting both the racial aggressiveness of whites and the passiveness of blacks. Because of his boldness and courage, Trotter is one of my great, but ignored, heroes of both black history and American history.

William Monroe Trotter was born in 1872. He was the first black student to become a member of the Phi Beta Kappa honor fraternity at Harvard—he was graduated as magna cum laude in 1895. In 1901 Trotter started a newspaper called *The Boston Guardian* which protested against discrimination.

In 1905 Trotter, along with W.E.B. DuBois, drafted the *Declaration of Principles* for the Niagara Movement, which later produced the NAACP. He wrote:

> "Persistent manly agitation is the way to liberty. We refuse to allow the impression to remain that the Negro American assents to inferiority."

Although it was very unpopular, even among blacks, Trotter practiced what he called, *agitation*, all his life. He spoke out against Booker T. Washington for encouraging blacks to accept various forms of discrimination, including the denial of their right to vote. (Washington's view was known as *accommodation*.)

Trotter was arrested once for trying to present his views at one of Booker T. Washington's speeches in Boston. The national press put Trotter down by calling his attempt to speak "The Boston Riot."

Trotter spoke out and worked against the popular movie *Birth of a Nation*. This film openly insulted black people and glorified KKK terrorism. (Sadly, but even today, *Birth of a Nation*, with all its racism, is still considered a great movie.)

In 1914 Trotter was invited to the White House to meet with President Woodrow Wilson. Wilson held strong racist views and had by Presidential order segregated the postal service based on skin-color. When Trotter asked President Wilson to share his views on racial segregation, Wilson replied to Trotter:

> "Segregation is not humbling but a benefit. Your manner offends me."

Then Trotter and Wilson had a strong discussion that lasted 45 minutes. The next day Trotter was attacked on the front page of *The New York Times for mistreating the president.*

In 1919 Trotter went to the Paris Peace Conference (which was to end World War I) in an effort to have them outlaw discrimination. The US State Department had denied him a passport, but he reached France anyway by working as a cook on a ship. There were no black delegates at the peace conference and his persistent efforts to be heard were continually denied.

Trotter died in 1934. With great financial and personal difficulty, he had published *The Boston*

Guardian as a voice for liberty for 33 years. Though not accepted in his times, many of William Monroe Trotter's methods were adopted in the 1950s by the Civil Rights Movement, especially his use of non-violent protest.

William Monroe Trotter once said:

> "I have finally given myself wholly to Christ to be led entirely by God. I have laid all my life, my business, my career, in the hands of Jesus and am to live and move in Him. Trust in Christ and then do what He tells you to at any cost. Don't trust in yourself, but in the power and help of God."

#8 - Ida B. Wells

> "The way to right wrongs is to turn the light of truth upon them." –Ida B. Wells

> "Virtue knows no color line." –Ida B. Wells

Ida B. Wells was born as a slave in Holly Springs, Mississippi in 1862 — six months before Abraham Lincoln's Emancipation Proclamation. At age 14 she became a school teacher. When she was 16 both her parents died of yellow fever. Ida B. Wells then moved to Memphis, Tennessee where she continued to teach school.

In 1884 Wells was ordered to move to the segregated Jim Crow car of a train. The 25-year old school teacher refused. Here's a quote from Ida B. Wells:

> "I refused. The conductor tried to drag me out of the seat, but the moment he caught hold of my arm I fastened my teeth on the back of his hand. He went forward and got the baggage man and another man to help him and of course they succeeded in dragging me out."

Wells hired an attorney in Memphis to sue the railroad. She won the case in the local court, but the Tennessee Supreme court reversed it and she had to pay $200.00 in court costs.

People wanted to know about her experience, so she began to write for black owned newspapers. Her editorials, critical of the inadequate black schools, caused her to lose her teaching job. Wells continued her writing and in 1889 she became a part owner of the Memphis newspaper: *Free Speech and Headlight*.

In 1892, three of Wells' friends were lynched in Memphis because a white grocer had lost customers to their grocery store. After the murder of her friends, Wells wrote:

> "There is only one thing for us to do; save our money and leave a town which will neither protect our lives and property, nor give us a fair trial in courts; but takes us out and murders us in cold blood when accused by white persons."

Then a mob burned down her paper's office. She was forced to leave Memphis under threat of her life.

Ida B. Wells settled in Chicago. In 1893 she published a pamphlet denouncing the exclusion of blacks from the Chicago World's Fair. She also wrote a book called: *Southern Horrors: Lynch Law in All its Phases*. Wells worked and wrote tirelessly against lynching, for women's right to vote, against the segregation of Chicago schools, and for many other just causes. She helped found several organizations, including the NAACP.

Wells is best known for her courageous work against lynching in America. Between 1880 and 1960, there were more than 4,000 documented lynchings in the USA. She wrote:

> "Brave men do not gather by the thousands to torture and murder a single individual, so gagged and bound he cannot make even feeble resistance or defense."

Throughout the years of public lynchings in America, the US government remained silent and passive. In 2005, the US Senate finally passed a resolution apologizing for not enacting anti-lynching legislation.

#7 - Robert Carter III

Robert Carter III of Virginia was one of the richest men in Revolutionary America. (He would have ranked near the top of the Forbes 400 List if they would have had one then.) He owned 16 plantations, 70,000 acres, numerous mansions, and several companies involved in shipping, manufacturing, and banking. He was the second largest slaveholder in Virginia "owning" more than 400 slaves.

Robert's fortune had been handed down to him from his grandfather and then his father. His grandfather had been so rich and powerful in Virginia that he had been given the nickname "King" Carter.

Robert was born in 1728. He was raised with wealth, privilege, and the Anglican religion. He enjoyed his lavish lifestyle until he was in his late 40s.

Two things, however, began to change him:

1) He was influenced by the ideas of personal freedom and liberty as the American colonists began to talk about independence from England. During the War of Independence, Carter sided with the revolutionaries. For Carter, however, it didn't make any sense to determine freedom by skin color. When the Declaration of Independence said, "*all men are created equal*," unlike many of the other American Founding Fathers, Carter began to believe what it really meant when it said **all** people, not just light skinned ones.

2) One of Carter's slaves was his own half-brother who was 3 years older than he and was referred to in Carter's journals as "Baptist Billy." In his late 40s Carter began to attend a very unusual Baptist church where slaves, free blacks, and whites worshiped together. On July 12, 1777, Robert Carter wrote in his journal:

> "I doubted till very lately of the divinity of Jesus Christ. I thank Almighty God that, that doubt is removed."

Another journal entry states:

> "On March 15, 1778, Robert Carter and his servant Negro Sam, received tokens and the both did Commune."

As Carter begin to enjoy a new relationship with some of his slaves as his brothers in Christ, his heart began to change toward them. Although still a slaveholder, he wrote in his journal:

> "Man is more than a mere inanimate statue."

And:

> "Tolerating slavery indicates great depravity."

As the founding fathers wrote eloquently about personal freedom, Carter tried to influence them to give freedom to the slaves of America. He wrote:

> "I apprehend that an act should pass here, declaring that all persons, male and female, were free from the date of the Act of Parliament declaring that the thirteen united states were free and independent states."

Eventually the northern states began to gradually free their slaves, but the southern states ignored his call. Carter later wrote:

> "My plans and advice have never been pleasing to the world."

Finally, in 1791 Carter acted independently, against the protests of many of his slaveholder friends. He wrote a document to provide freedom to all of his 442 slaves called *The Deed of Gift* and filed it with the state of Virginia. He began by saying:

> "I have for some time past been convinced that to retain persons in Slavery is contrary to the true Principles of Religion and Justice, and therefore it was my Duty to manumit them."

This was by far the largest number of slaves ever set free by an individual in American history. Carter also liquidated most of his fortune and gave each slave he freed a significant amount of money.

Later that year, John Rippon wrote in a newspaper called *Baptist Register*:

> "It is said that Mr. Robert Carter of Nomini, Virginia has emancipated 442 slaves, if this be true, vote him a triumph, crown him with laurels, and let millions listen while he sings — *'I would not have a slave to till my ground.'*"

Instead of listening to Carter, America ignored and forgot him and his wonderful document of freedom — *The Deed of Gift*. He was even persecuted in his home state and finally forced to move out of Virginia. So, he moved to Baltimore.

Robert Carter was one of America's greatest Founding Father because he applied the principles of freedom to all people (not just to white people) and because he believed **all lives matter including black lives**. Had his example been followed by the other Founding Fathers, American history would have been radically changed and millions of Americans would not have had to suffer the cruel drudgery, bondage, and torture of slavery.

#6 - The Grimke Sisters

> "I am persuaded that the rights of woman, like the rights of slaves, need only be examined to be understood and asserted." –Sarah Grimke

> "Human beings have rights because they are moral beings; the rights of all men grow out of their moral nature; and as all men have the same moral nature, they have essentially the same rights. These rights may be wrestled from the slave, but they cannot be alienated: his title to himself is stamped on his moral being and is, like it, imperishable." –Angelina Grimke

Two sisters, daughters of a prominent South Carolina plantation owner and judge are my #6 greatest Americans. Their names are Sarah Grimke (1792-1873) and Angelina Grimke (1805-1879).

At age 5 Sarah saw a slave being wiped so she tried to board a steam boat, so she could live in a place where there was no such thing as slavery. A few years later Sarah tried to teach her slave companion and "maid" to read. Sarah said:

"The light was put out, the keyhole screened, and flat on our stomachs, before the fire, with the spelling book under our eyes, we defied the laws of South Carolina."

Sarah was caught and punished. Sarah was very bright, but she was forbidden a formal education by her father because she was a girl.

Thirteen years younger, Angelina grew up being cared for by Sarah. She also was very sensitive to the pain and injustice being suffered by the slaves on their father's plantation.

As a young adult Sarah moved to the North and Angelina eventually followed her. There, the sisters began to work and speak against slavery. Angelina wrote an anti-slavery letter to William Lloyd Garrison which was published in *The Liberator*, the major abolitionist newspaper in America. This opened the door for the sisters to become the first female speakers for the Anti-Slavery Society.

As they traveled throughout the North sharing their first-hand experiences of the cruelty of slavery, their lectures received violent criticism because it was considered improper (politically incorrect) for women to speak out on political issues. The sisters had started out speaking up for the human rights of others but wound up also fighting for their own rights as women.

In 1838, Angelina presented an anti-slavery petition signed by 20,000 women to the Massachusetts legislature becoming the first woman in American history ever to address a state legislature. Afterward she said:

> "Our Lord and Master gave me His arm to lean upon and in great weakness my limbs trembling under me, I stood up and spoke."

This is part of what Angelina said that day:

> "I stand before you as a Southerner, exiled from the land of my birth by the sound of the lash and the piteous cry of the slave. I stand before you as a repentant slaveholder. As a moral being I feel I owe it to the suffering slave and to the deluded master, to my country and to the world to do all that I can to overturn a system of complicated crimes."

Both sisters boldly wrote and published widely distributed books against slavery, for women's rights, and against racism. Sarah wrote: *Epistle to the Clergy of the Southern States* and *Letters on the Equality of The Sexes*. Angelina wrote: *Appeal to the Christian Women of the South* and *Appeal to the Women of the Nominally Free States*.

After the Civil War the sisters discovered that they had three "colored" nephews. Their brother, Henry Grimke had fathered three sons by his slave, Mary Weston. When Henry died, the sisters invited their nephews north and embraced them as family. They helped them financially and had a close relationship with two of them, Francis Grimke and Archibald Grimke—both of whom became famous civil rights leaders. Archibald even named his daughter "Angelina."

#5 - U.S. Senator Charles Sumner

Charles Sumner was elected to the US Senate in 1851 and served until his death in 1874. He believed in equal rights for all and continually spoke out strongly against slavery on the Senate floor saying things like:

> "Slavery is odious as an institution, if viewed in the light of morals and Christianity."

And:

> "Where slavery is liberty cannot be; and where liberty is slavery cannot be."

Historians consider him "the Senate's leading opponent of slavery." Because of this, Charles Sumner was hated by many people.

On May 22, 1856, Senator Sumner was beaten unconscious with a cane on the Senate floor by Preston Brooks, a member of the US House of Representatives, because of his anti-slavery stand. Sumner's severe injuries kept him away from his Senate duties for three years, until December 1859.

On his return to the Senate he continued to work for the end of slavery and equal rights for all. After the Civil War, Sumner led the "radicals" in the Senate who wanted to give citizenship and voting rights to the freed slaves. He boldly advocated color-kindness by saying:

> "It will do us no good to make the blacks as free as the whites unless we learn to have good feelings toward them and treat them well."

Due mainly to Sumner's bold influence in the Senate and Thaddeus Stevens' influence in the House of Representatives, three "Civil Rights" amendments were added to the US Constitution, officially giving blacks citizenship, voting rights, and equal rights under the law.

Although these amendments were gradually set aside and made ineffective by the Supreme Court, leading to almost a century of segregation, racial terrorism, and Jim Crow laws, they remained in the Constitution. When the Civil Rights movement began in earnest in the 1950s, the leaders had Constitutional rights to stand on, thanks in large part to the moral courage of Charles Sumner—my fifth greatest American.

Sumner said:

> "It is never too late to do right."

And:

> "By the law of slavery, man, created in the image of God, is divested of human character and declared to be a mere chattel."

#4 - U.S. Congressman Thaddeus Stevens

Thaddeus Stevens was born in 1792 in Vermont to a poor family and was abandoned by his father at an early age. He was handicapped from birth because of a club foot. When he was a child all his hair fell out, and from then onward he wore a wig.

Thaddeus Stevens moved to Pennsylvania at age twenty-two and became a prominent lawyer at Gettysburg and then at Lancaster. He was elected to the U.S. Congress in 1848, 1850, and again in 1858 where he served until his death in 1868.

During Stevens' lifetime, extreme racial prejudice was rampant in America. Only a couple of Northern States allowed blacks to vote. Despite the beautiful phrase in the Declaration of Independence which says: "all men are created equal"—strict segregation and harsh discrimination were practiced throughout the North, and the sentence of lifetime forced labor and human bondage in the South. Those who dared to speak out for human rights for blacks were persecuted in the North and driven out or killed in the South.

Yet, Stevens from his early adulthood went against the tide of public opinion and stood firmly and boldly against both slavery and prejudice. He said:

> "This is not a white man's government! To say so is political blasphemy, for it violates the fundamental principles of our gospel of liberty."

Despite his stand, Stevens became very powerful in Congress.

When the first Congress met after the Civil War had ended, the Southern states sent representatives and senators to Washington expecting them to be seated in Congress. The men they sent were mostly former Confederate office holders.

American President Andrew Johnson and much of Congress thought they should be accepted back and seated. But not Thaddeus Stevens.

Stevens was greatly concerned about leaving three million freed slaves under the political control of their former masters. He knew if the Congress seated the former Confederates, the freed blacks in the South would never get equal rights.

So, Stevens and the man who called the roll in Congress left out the names of the Southern representatives when the role was called and refused to seat them.

Also, as the former Confederate states began to write new state constitutions to be readmitted to the Union, they included "black codes" which strongly discriminated against and persecuted the freed slaves. President Johnson agreed with the "black codes." But not Stevens.

As the movie, *Lincoln*, shows; Thaddeus Stevens helped Abraham Lincoln get the 13th Amendment (that permanently ended slavery in the United States) through Congress. Then Stevens almost single-handedly influenced Congress to pass several laws and constitutional amendments providing citizenship and equal rights and voting right to blacks.

Stevens influenced Congress to require that Southern states agree with these laws before they could be readmitted to the Union. This opened the way for blacks to be involved in politics in the South. Several blacks became US Senators and Congressmen.

White Southerners hated Thaddeus Stevens and his courageous accomplishments for human rights. They violently opposed black freedom and eventually stopped blacks from voting, ignored the equal-rights Constitutional Amendments, set up Jim Crow laws which separated blacks from whites, and enforced them through the illegal terrorism of the KKK and other vigilante groups.

However, in the 1950s and '60s blacks once again asserted their freedom. The laws and amendments Stevens led through Congress were the legal backbone for the demands of the modern Civil Rights Movement. Thus, this courageous man helped give freedom to many millions of Americans.

Thaddeus Stevens stood for equal rights 'til his death. He was buried in a black cemetery. His tombstone says:

> "I repose in this quiet and secluded spot. Not from any natural preference for solitude, but, finding other Cemeteries limited as to Race by Charter Rules, I have chosen this that I might illustrate in my death, The Principles which I advocated Through a long life; EQAULITY OF

MAN BEFORE HIS CREATOR."

#3 - William J. Seymour

William J. Seymour is my third greatest American of all time. He was born in 1870 in Centerville, Louisiana to former slaves. He grew up during great poverty and racism. He had little education although he did teach himself to read. He became a believer in Christ at a young age and moved to Houston, TX as an evangelist in 1903.

While living in Houston, Seymour met Charles F. Parham, a white evangelist from Topeka, KS who in 1901, along with a small group of Bible school students, had experienced the ancient Christian gift of speaking in tongues. Parham had been preaching about this gift ever since but had received very limited interest from people.

Parham had started a Bible school in Houston which William J. Seymour wanted to attend. Because Parham and his students were white, Seymour had to sit outside the classroom listening through an open door because of the racist Jim Crow laws of that time.

In January 1906, William J. Seymour was invited to pastor a small, black, holiness church in Los Angeles, California. Although Seymour had not yet experienced speaking in tongues, he, nevertheless, began preaching the gift of speaking in tongues was for today; consequently, he was asked to leave the church.

On April 9, 1906, William Seymour prayed for a friend to be healed of an illness—the friend began to speak in tongues. That night Seymour held a meeting in a private home; seven people began to speak in tongues. As the news spread, crowds began to gather as more and more people began to speak in tongues.

As their numbers grew, they needed a larger place to meet, so they rented an old church building at 312 Azusa Street. The building had most recently been used as a horse stable. For the next three years services were held there three times a day, every day, at 10:00 am, noon, and 7:00 pm. The crowds grew to 700-800 people inside the building with several hundred more people outside for each meeting. The meetings were multi-racial and international, as people flocked to Azusa Street from all over America—all over the world.

As thousands experienced the Christian gift of speaking in tongues, their love and passion for Jesus soared to high levels. Many missionaries left Azusa Street and went to countries around the world. They were known as "missionaries of the one-way ticket" because they went to stay to show God's love. Many other people went back to their home towns and spread "the message of Pentecost."

William J. Seymour preached the main sign of the "Pentecostal experience" was not tongues, but heart-felt love and compassion for all people. In a time when it was illegal for races to meet in most of America, Azusa Street attracted all races. Seymour began to publish a newspaper called *The Apostolic*

Faith and it quickly grew to 50,000 in circulation. The paper did not use by-lines and listed no editor, as "Seymour wanted himself and others to keep a low profile, so God could get all the glory!"

Seymour and others who led and attended Azusa Street received much persecution. In September 1906, the <u>Los Angeles Times</u> wrote:

> "Disgraceful intermingling of the races. They have a one-eyed illiterate Negro (Seymour) as their preacher who stays on his knees much of the time with his head hidden between wooden crates."

Seymour's attitude was:

> "No instrument that God can use is rejected on account of color or dress or lack of education."

After three years, the persecution and attacks against Seymour and Azusa Street began to have an effect and the crowds gradually began to drop off. Seymour continued to pastor the Azusa Street Mission until his death in 1922. By that time only a handful of members remained.

So why is William J. Seymour my third greatest American of all time? Because of the worldwide impact of his ministry and of the Azusa Street Revival. When Seymour received the Pentecostal experience only a few thousand people in the world had received it. Through Azusa Street tens of thousands of people received it and spread it all around the world. Today it is estimated that more than 500 million people (of all Christian denominations) speak in tongues. All Pentecostals and charismatics trace their history back to the bold, multiracial meetings at Azusa Street.

Azusa Street was never segregated by race and most of the early Pentecostal groups were interracial. However, eventually the forced segregation in American society overcame the color unity of the Pentecostal movement and divided it along color lines. Had those groups remained multi-racial, America's race problems might have been overcome years ago.

#2 - Martin Luther King, Jr.

King was born into a family of black ministers in 1929 in Atlanta, Georgia. He received a bachelor's degree in sociology from Morehouse College when only 19 years old. He went on to get a master's degree from Crozer Theological Seminary in Chester, PA where he was the first black student body president and graduated first in his class. Next, he earned a Ph.D. in systematic theology from Boston University in 1955, where he met and married Coretta Scott.

After his education he became pastor of Dexter Avenue Baptist Church in Montgomery, Alabama in 1955. In December of that year, Rosa Parks was arrested for refusing to give her seat on a bus to a white man.

The black citizens of Montgomery then formed the Montgomery Improvement Association with King as head. This organization then began a bus boycott which lasted more than a year during which King's life was repeatedly threatened, and his home was bombed. The boycott forced Montgomery and the bus company to desegregate the buses. In late 1957 the Supreme Court declared the bus segregation law to be unconstitutional.

Afterward, King worked tirelessly leading civil rights marches and protests across the South and around America. He elevated the idea of equal rights into a moral movement by appealing to the conscience of the nation. His use of nonviolent resistance captured the country's sympathy due to the violence and brutality directed at non-violent protesters. Martin Luther King, Jr.'s speeches rang with passion, commitment, and justice as they stirred the souls of millions of people across America.

In 1964 King was awarded the Nobel Peace Prize. King was the first black American to be named *Time* magazine's "Man of the Year." His efforts and the efforts of tens of thousands of other brave Americans led to the end of legal racial discrimination in employment, desegregation of public places, and the enforcement of voting rights for blacks and other minorities. King paid the ultimate price for freedom when he was murdered in Memphis, TN in 1968 because of his work for "liberty and justice for all."

#1 - William Lloyd Garrison

William Lloyd Garrison was born to a poor family in

1805. As a young man he met Benjamin Lundy, who published a newspaper called, the *Genius of Universal Emancipation* and was almost single-handedly speaking out against slavery. Garrison began to work with Lundy and caught a heart-felt vision for liberty and justice for all Americans. He began to work passionately and tirelessly for freedom for the slaves, which was a very unpopular cause at the time in the North. He insisted on immediate emancipation.

Garrison and a few others founded the Anti-Slavery Society which gradually grew to have a wide influence. In 1831 he began to publish the *Liberator*, a weekly anti-slavery newspaper which at great financial sacrifice, he published until all the slaves were freed in 1865.

This caused Garrison to be hated across America. He was almost killed by a pro-slavery mob in his home town of Boston. Almost every day he received letters containing threats of violence against him. The state of Georgia even put a $5000 price on his head, *dead or alive.*

Garrison, through his non-religious Christian faith held to his view of non-violent resistance. He believed in using persuasion (which he called "*moral suasion*") rather than violence. He saw slavery for the terrible crime it was and boldly spoke out against it no matter what it personally cost him. With fiery words, a prophet's passion, and a hero's courage he forced the country to face its most crucial moral issue—the act of forcibly holding three million innocent men, women, and children in lifelong servitude, bondage, and degradation, while proclaiming human freedom.

My greatest American has been mostly brushed aside by historians or pictured as a crazy radical. His greatness for the most part has been missed by American historians. But Russian novelist, Leo Tolstoy, was strongly influenced by Garrison's untiring work for justice through non-violent direct action. He wrote about it in his book, *The Kingdom of God.*"

An Indian man named Gandhi read Tolstoy's book and adopted Garrison's non-violent direct action using it to free the nation of India from British control.

Then a Southern American pastor, Martin Luther King, Jr., went to India to visit Mahatma Gandhi and adopted non-violent direct action as the cornerstone for the American Civil Rights Movement.

William Lloyd Garrison is my hero. Oh, that we had more people like him today. A wonderful biography of Garrison is: *All on Fire,* by Henry Mayer.

Two of My 21st Century American Heroes

White people used to make black people go to their back door. Today, many white people never even invite black people to their home at all. However, my heroes, Thom and Michele Hazelip, are a white couple who turned their own front porch into an inner-city community gathering place—a place of love, compassion, liberty, and justice for all.

In 2004 Thom and Michele Hazelip bought a run-down investment house that backed up to a large, low-income apartment complex in inner-city Nashville, Tennessee. At the time it was a very violent neighborhood. As Thom began to repair the house, he began to get to know people in the neighborhood. He met kids who didn't have an advocate and who didn't believe things could ever change. He met parents who were overwhelmed while doing their best just to cope with difficult situations and circumstances.

Soon he and Michele realized their house wasn't just an investment property, but a home for them to live in; a place to raise their family, and an opportunity to make a difference in a neighborhood of hurting people. So, they moved in with their two kids (now they have four), and opened their home, and front porch, to the area's at-risk kids and moms. Today, Front Porch Ministry is about living in friendship and open, caring relationships with the underserved community they reside in.

Thom puts it this way:

> "We thought we were just moving nine miles from our home, and it turns out, the more people that we met and got involved with down here; the more it feels like we are in a totally different country–a country that's near America—but a country that thinks very differently from how I grew up or the world I grew up in. Because of that, we began to understand, this is where we

need to go, and this is where we need to help out."

Ernie and I worked with The Salvation Army in the same neighborhood from 2005 to 2017 and have seen firsthand the powerful impact this couple and their children have made. They have continually sponsored and led activities for neighborhood kids and their moms on their front porch and in their yard—everything from movies, to ice cream parties, to basketball, to crafts, to holiday events, to free food trucks, and much more. They have personally tutored and/or mentored many children and their moms too numerous to count.

Thom and Michele have opened their home and fed many neighborhood people at their family meals. They have opened their door in the middle of the night to people. They have let children and teenagers spend the night with them and even live with them.

Over the years, they have brought in hundreds of volunteers who have personally served and helped people in the community in numerous ways. Thom and Michele have helped many people financially giving neighborhood people the opportunity to earn money working with them.

Mostly, Thom and Michele and their four kids, have shown unceasing and unconditional love. Ernie and I once took a high-ranking Salvation Army leader to tour Thom and Michele's front porch and home. There were kids and teenagers (and even a few moms) all over the house. Thom and Michele showed us the community food pantry, the teen room, the backyard sports area and more. They told stories about some of the amazing things they had experienced while serving others. As we left, The Salvation Army leader turned to Ernie and me and said, "I don't know anybody else who would do what they're doing."

Maybe their story will inspire you to show more love across racial lines. If you would like to know more about them, search for *Front Porch Ministry* on the web or on Facebook. They would love for you to get involved in person and/or financially and connecting with them will be an amazing blessing for you.

So, what motivates Thom and Michele? Thom says:

> "I hope, years from now I can look back and see boys that turned into men but did not keep the same pattern that was in their mom's life or in the lives of the men that came in and out of their home. I hope our being here means that people feel they have an advocate, a friend—somebody who walks through life with them, leads them through the trials and tragedies and triumphs. I hope they know that they're not alone and that they hopefully will be pointed to Jesus."

My Top 10 Greatest Americans

4. Early Jewish, Christian, Jesus' Views on Race

More of My Original Thinking About Race

When we're conceived in the womb, the dye is cast; our coloring is automatically delivered by our DNA. Color is an accident of birth. (We weren't allowed to pick our color.) So why should one color of accident at birth mean any more than another? Color difference doesn't necessitate division.

To appreciate human skin coloration, perhaps we could replace race with grace. Perhaps our modern racial problems need ancient, *gracial* solutions. Maybe *gracism* can *erase* racism.

To focus on skin-differences instead of on shared human similarities is to invite unnecessary disagreement and conflict. Skin color reactions, far too often, prevent people from knowing each other heart-to-heart.

Ancient Views of Skin Color

In the ancient world, there was no skin-color hierarchy. No shade of skin was inferior or seen as a badge of shame.

Prior to the modern era, humans didn't even classify and divide people according to their skin color; but by religion, class, language, tribe, ethnicity, etc. Although they noticed the differences in people's skin, they didn't think of it as a meaningful way to sort people into groups. For example, in ancient

Greece and Rome, whether people were slave or free had nothing to do with their appearance. People were enslaved because of conquest or debt, but not because of physical characteristics like skin color.

Perhaps the ancients were right, and we moderns are wrong. Most of the physical traits of human beings come from inheriting individual genes, not from being grouped into something called race. Different groups of humans have interbred throughout our history. We are all mixed and there is no clearly distinct race of people. People who have had their ancestry traced through their DNA discover the reality of that statement. We all have diverse ancestry if you go back far enough. In other words, we are all like *Heinz 57 Sauce* with ingredients from lots of *colorly* diverse ancestors.

People's skin tone seems to be determined by the amount of sunlight their ancestors were exposed to and the latitude their ancestors lived in, but not by race. Race is a social construct, not a physiological one. I read somewhere there are more genetic differences in a single group of chimpanzees in a forest somewhere, than in the entire human race.

The Jewish Version Colorblind Racism

The Jewish view of race was completely colorblind. It had nothing at all to do with skin color. When the Jews looked at the world they saw two races, themselves and everybody else—Jews and Gentiles—and they practiced segregation from the Gentiles. (Jews weren't even allowed to eat with Gentiles or to go into a Gentile home.) However, the most despised group to the Jews was a small group of mixed people between the two races called *Samaritans*.

In ancient times, the Jewish nation of Israel split into two countries; the northern kingdom of Israel (ten of the twelve tribes of Israel) and the southern kingdom of Judah (the tribes of Judah and Benjamin). Eventually the powerful kingdom of Assyria conquered the kingdom of Israel and hauled off most of the Israelites who belonged to the ten tribes of northern Israel into captivity.

Those ten northern tribes were assimilated into the cultures where the Assyrians forcibly dispersed them, and they disappeared from history. They are known as "the ten lost tribes of Israel." However, some members of the ten tribes (the very poor) were left in northern Israel and interbred with foreigners whom the Assyrians brought into their land. This produced a new group of people of mixed Israelite and Gentile ancestry called Samaritans.

Jews (those of Judah) practiced hyper-segregation against the Samaritans (even though, like black Americans, their despised racial identity wasn't their fault). The Jews had no dealings with the Samaritans. In Jesus' time Jews lived in Judea and Galilee, on the northern and southern sides of Samaria. To avoid contact with the Samaritans, Jews refused to go into their neighborhoods. Rather than going directly through Samaria to get to Judea or Galilee, Jews would take a much longer route encircling Samaria by crossing the Jordan river twice. (None of this was based on color because the

Jews and the Samaritans were basically the same color.)

Jesus Christ, however, broke the Jewish, color-blind racial tradition of avoiding and ignoring the Samaritans. Rather than insulting them, Jesus talked compassionately about Samaritans to His fellow Jews. He even told a story about a man (probably a Jew) who was robbed, beaten, and left on the side of the road.

A Jewish priest and a Levite both walked by the injured man and ignored him. Then a Samaritan came along and had compassion (not racial-blindness, but racial-kindness) on the man. He bandaged the injured man, took him to an inn, and gave the innkeeper money to take care of the injured man. He told the innkeeper that if he needed more money, he would cover it when he returned.

Then Jesus told those listening to "Go and do the same." In other words, be like that heroic, kind, and noble "Good Samaritan." (Perhaps it's time for all colors in America to begin to get to know the many heroic, kind, and noble blacks, and other colors, who have been left out of our history.)

When Jesus and His disciples would transverse between Judea and Galilee (which they did several times), He would always violate Jewish racial protocol while openly walking right through the *Samaritan hood*.

Once when He stopped at a well in Samaria, His

disciples went for food and left Him alone at the well. Then Jesus saw a Samaritan woman and began a kind and friendly conversation with her. When His disciples returned they were shocked that Jesus would violate the segregation rules and have a conversation with a Samaritan and a woman.

The woman went back to her village and told everybody about her conversation with a Jew named Jesus. Then the Samaritans from that village went to Jesus and asked Him to stay with them a few days. (It warms people's hearts when you ignore racial traditions and go out of your way to meet them while showing them kindness.) Jesus stayed with them and socialized with them for a few days, violating the non-biblical, Jewish segregation laws. He went beyond racial blindness by noticing Samaritans through talking about them, honoring them, talking with them, and socializing with them.

When was the last time you hung out with someone who society says you shouldn't like? Try it.

White as a Sheet Full of Animals

Being Jewish, the first Christians initially struggled with racism which had nothing to do with color. They reached out to their fellow Jews and welcomed them into the growing Christian community which grew to more than 8,000 Jewish Christ-followers in the city of Jerusalem. However, they mainly avoided and ignored the *Gentiles* (i.e., those from the "nations" or the ethnos [Greek for "ethnic groups"]).

Then the religious Jews in Jerusalem became jealous of the growing Christian movement and began to persecute them intensely and violently. After a Jewish Christ-follower named Steven was murdered for his faith, nearly all the Christians fled Jerusalem and scattered all across the territory of Judea. Some crossed the border into Samaria and before they knew it, Samaritans began to follow Christ, so the Jewish believers in Christ reluctantly received them. However, no Christians had yet reached out to the pagan Gentiles.

Then one day a Roman commander of a hundred men (called a centurion), whose name was Cornelius, had a vision. He saw an angel who told him to send men to the city of Joppa to bring back a man called Simon Peter who was staying in a house by the sea—he did so.

The following day, Simon Peter, one of Jesus' boldest followers, was resting on a rooftop deck when he fell into a trance and saw a huge sheet full of all sorts of animals the Jews were forbidden to eat. Then he heard a voice say: "Take up, Peter. Kill and eat." But Peter responded to the voice; "Surely not, Lord! I have never eaten anything impure or unclean."

The voice spoke to Peter a second time and said: "Do not call anything impure that God has made clean." Then, two more times, Peter saw the sheet full of animals that were forbidden by the Jews to eat; and heard the voice say the same thing. Both times he argued with the voice.

As Peter was still wondering about the meaning of the sheet full of unclean animals, God spoke to him and said: "Three men are looking for you. So, get up and go downstairs. Do not hesitate to go with them for I have sent them."

Suddenly, at that moment, the men from Cornelius knocked on the door downstairs. They asked for Peter.

Then Peter and a few others went with them back to Cornelius' house. Cornelius had invited a group from his household to wait for Peter with him. Peter said to them: "You are well aware that it is against our law for a Jew to associate with or visit a Gentile. But God has shown me that I should not call anyone impure or unclean. So, when I was sent for, I came."

Peter went on to say: "I now realize how true it is that God does not show favoritism but accepts from ***every nation*** the one who fears Him and does what is right." As Peter told them about Jesus Christ, the Spirit of God fell on the Gentiles in Cornelius' house and the Jewish believers with Peter were amazed because they saw God working among the nations. This opened the door for First Century Christianity to go beyond the Jewish, two-race system and to unite Jews and those from the nations into what was later called: One New Man.

Early *Gracist* Community of Reconciliation & Unity

The early Christians began to teach the *wall of separation* between Jews and the Nations had been torn down by Christ. They taught that Christ, with His blood, *"purchased for God persons from every tribe and language and people and nation."* Therefore, they welcomed people of any color or ethnic group to come and follow Christ in intimate, interactive, informal community with them.

The early Christ-followers truly saw all people as equal before God and before one another. They met in an open forum where anybody present could speak up in any given meeting. Paul, one of the primary writers of the New Testament describes their meetings like this: *"When you come together, each of you has a hymn, or a word of instruction, a revelation, a tongue or an interpretation."*

Rather than looking to a leadership hierarchy, they learned to serve each other in humble mutuality. There are more than 50 places in the New Testament where the early Christ-followers are instructed to do things like; *"love one another," "teach one another," "confess your faults to one another," "bear one another's burdens," "encourage one another," "don't bite, devour, and consume one another," "be kind, tender-hearted, and forgiving to one another," "seek good for one another and don't repay evil for evil," "serve one another," "give preference to one another," "don't lie to one another," "be hospitable to one another," "pray for one another,"* etc.

If we would begin to live out this early lifestyle of *gracist* Christianity, it would go a very long way toward healing America's racial wounds. Unfortunately, the history of racial cruelties committed by many who called themselves Christians and the active support and justification for color-based slavery (that is completely unknown in the Bible) along with discrimination by much of the Christian church, often made American Christianity to appear as an ally of racial injustice rather than a *gracial* antidote to it.

Fortunately, as we have seen, throughout American history there were also courageous Christ-followers (both white and black) who went against the tide of racial injustice while boldly standing up for God-given human rights for all people. Most of the American Abolitionists (people who were activists for ending slavery) were motivated by a personal relationship with Christ. Also, the Civil Rights Movement had a strong foundation based upon the truths of Christianity. Here's an example of a *gracially* motivated, American Civil Rights leader.

Questions for Civil Rights Leader, Ralph Abernathy

Famous Civil Rights leader, Ralph Abernathy, was a campus speaker when I was in college. In a packed ballroom he told his audience about his experiences in the Civil Rights Movement while working with Dr. Martin Luther King, Jr.

After his lecture, he asked if there were any questions. I threw my hand up and he picked me. I asked: "Rev. Abernathy, would you please tell us how you came to know Jesus Christ as your personal Savior?"

Rev. Abernathy seemed a bit startled by my question. He paused, then he said something like this:

> "When I was a young boy I went to the altar one Sunday morning in my father's Baptist church and there I met Jesus Christ. And I've never been the same."

Then he got excited. He sounded like he was preaching from the pulpit in that special black-church style. For five minutes or so he boldly declared his love for Jesus Christ.

After we were dismissed, several angry people rushed up to me. One guy said: "Why did you ask him THAT?" "I was curious," I said.

Another firmly stated: "He wasn't here for THAT!" I replied, "He didn't have to answer my question." However, I am sure glad he did. Even today, as I remember Ralph Abernathy's passion for Jesus Christ, I am inspired! Many of the Civil Rights Leaders were inspired by THAT.

America's Divided Churches

Should churches which represent Heaven and all of its glorious human diversity (people from "every kindred and every tribe") be able to be identified by the prominent skin color of the people who attend? For example, in the USA, we have black churches, white churches, red (Native American) churches, brown (Hispanic) churches, and yellow (Asian) churches.

Many years after the end of government sponsored and enforced racial segregation the Christian churches in American are still some of the most segregated places in our nation. And most people are not bothered by that fact. In fact, the popular *church growth movement* taught multitudes of churches and Christian leaders that churches grow better when they are segregated by race, ethnicity, economic status, and/or skin color.

The truth is, however, segregated churches are a contradiction of the place they claim to represent: Heaven (and the kingdom of God). Paul taught Jesus tore down the "wall of partition" between Jews and Gentiles—people who were divided should now be united in Christ.

For Christians to worship primarily with people who have the same color of skin as they do has always seemed to me to be a denial of God's healing and reconciling power. The glory and power of the Gospel is shown not when people assemble with people who look like them, but when people worship with and love people from across racial lines humans have drawn.

Anybody can gather with people like them. However, it takes the supernatural love and power of God to gather with and love people you have been taught not to appreciate.

We Americans need to finally tear down the walls in our churches and unite in love with believers of different skin shades than our own. Then the world will be able to see that our belief in Jesus is real and not just rusty ritual.

My daughter and her cousin taught me a lesson about this when they were both about 4 years old. Ernie and I told them we were going to take them to a black church. When we all got out of the car, one of them said: "That's not a black church, it's a red brick church."

> "Was not Jesus an extremist for love? . . .. The question is not whether we will be extremists, but what kind of extremists we will be." –Martin Luther King, Jr.

Torah-fying For Healing?

We need the truth to set us free from false concepts of race! Perhaps it is time to break our civil commandment: "You shall not look too closely at the racial injustices in American history." Being unaware of the details of racial wrongs in our history is not good for any group—not blacks, not Native Americans, not Hispanics, not Asians, not recent immigrants, and not even for whites.

Yet, don't all countries "tidy up" their history? Almost all do. However, there is one country that has a history book that openly declares and exposes the evil in their past. It honestly reveals and displays the wrongdoing of even their greatest leaders. It's called the Torah—it tells the story of ancient Israel.

The Torah boldly exposes the wrongdoing of the

Patriarchs of Israel, their founding fathers. It gives the details of Abraham's lies; of Isaac's being deceived; of Jacob's lies and deceptions; of Jacob's 12 sons (the founders of the 12 tribes of Israel) selling one of their brothers into slavery, then deceiving Jacob into believing the boy, Joseph, had been killed by a wild animal. It tells how two of Jacob's sons made a deceptive peace treaty with a village—then came back and murdered all the men of that village. It tells how another of Jacob's sons impregnated his daughter-in-law, thinking she was a prostitute, and then threatened to kill her when he found out she was pregnant.

The Torah gives the details of Moses killing an Egyptian. It also openly reveals the racism of Miriam (Moses' sister) and Aaron (his brother) both of whom criticized him because he was married to an Ethiopian woman. (The fact that it doesn't mention his wife's color, which would have been black, once again shows that the idea of race wasn't based on color in the ancient world.)

The Jewish history books reveal how David committed adultery, and then committed murder to cover it up. They openly admit to and describe in detail much wrongdoing by the nations of Israel and Judah, even how they would sometimes kill their own children as human sacrifices to pagan idols. The writings of the Jewish prophets strongly rebuke both Judah and Israel while holding them accountable for their wrongdoing as well as for the wrongdoing of their forefathers.

Perhaps we could Torah-fy American history.

Perhaps we could look beyond the myths and begin to openly admit the painful details of our forefathers' wrongful deeds. But why? Because we need truth to heal and move forward. The concept of race is still a big problem in America. We need truth to heal.

That's why South Africa held an ongoing Truth And Reconciliation Commission. They wanted to discover and reveal past wrongdoing by the government, by groups, and by individuals, so they could resolve conflict left over from the past by asking for and receiving forgiveness. America never did that, not after emancipation and not after the Civil Rights Movement. We just moved on in denial, without "truth and reconciliation."

Perhaps it is not too late. We could begin by replacing some historical terms that serve as a smokescreen for truth. Here are some examples: We could replace slavery with human trafficking, slave owner with human trafficker, Indian removal with genocide, segregation with apartheid, Indian treaties with land grabs, night riders with terrorists, runaways with freedom fighters, slave revolts with revolutionary heroes, plantations with forced-labor camps. Plus, we could bring to light the horrid details of some of the unmentionables like lynchings, lashings, torture devices, rape, men enslaving their own children, etc.

If we can't openly and honestly discuss the problem of race (even if it makes our forefathers look bad) how can we ever solve it? Perhaps it's too easy for us white people, who were not the active victims of extreme racial cruelty, to ignore the past and current-day consequences of racial injustice in America! I sure did. It is so easy to presume racial innocence of ourselves and our forefathers.

5. Short History on White/Black Interaction

Some of My Original Thoughts About History

Flowers of different colors make a bouquet. People of different colors have far too often made a mess! America still hasn't recovered from the skin-color cancer that it created and ignored for centuries. However, it's still possible to take all the pieces of a divided America and make an amazing mosaic.

Instead of seeing darker skin color as part of a beautiful human collage, the early American colonists began to define it as a sign of inferiority. Early in its history, colonial America had a huge infusion of color exclusion laws.

Today, after centuries of color-based insults, violence, abuse, and dominance, we've made talking about skin color a taboo; something people aren't supposed to do. Perhaps it's time for open, honest talk about America's history of color prejudice.

For centuries in America, noticing skin-color was a hate-fest. Black skin color was a public badge of dishonor. It was openly talked about and written about in derogatory ways. It was an excuse to look down on people, control them, use them, and forcibly reject them from society. Unfortunately, even today some people (and, tragically, police officers) still see blackness as a probable cause wherein criminal activity may have taken or is taking place.

Black History Is American History

Some people say that we shouldn't talk about black history in the USA, just American history. But surely, every American's story deserves to be told. When we honestly look back at America's past, skin color was a really big deal and America's policies were not only not color-kind, they were color-cruel.

People with lighter skins were favored by government and institutions, even by the Constitution. People with darker skins were considered to be less than human, had no legal rights, and could be legally abused and forcibly held in life long bondage even though they had committed no crime.

The legacy of this history of great inequality still affects the psyche of Americans in spite of our attempts to ignore it and pretend it never happened. Perhaps, it is time to accept black history into American history and as Paul Harvey used to say; teach and tell "the rest of the story." After all, the whole story of America, the full experience of whites, blacks, Native Americans and other ethnic groups is the one history of our country.

Why A White Guy Digs into Black History

That being said: I like to read black history as an adult, because I was never taught that part of American history in school. Every month is black history month to me. I dig into all the black history I can find. When I tell people I am into reading and

studying black history, they usually look at me with a puzzled look and ask "Why?" ... as if to say: "What's a white guy doing that for?"
Here are some of my reasons:

1) I find most of the black history makers to be amazing people who overcame almost impossible odds. For example, men and women who were held by intimidation and violence in forced bondage, denied any education, and treated like animals— courageously found ways to survive with minimal hatred. Many found ways to escape and to tell (and write) their stories.

2) Black history reveals many cruel secrets of American history, what I call hidden history. Without black (and other minority) history, American history is whitewashed and incomplete. I want to know the whole story of American history, not just the parts that make America look good.

3) As a white guy, I want to understand the full American experience, not just my own or the experience of people with a similar skin shade to mine. I want to, as much as I can, learn from the American experiences of others.

4) To ignore black history is a form of denial—a pretending that it didn't happen or that it was irrelevant.

5) I find black history both inspiring and heart-rending. The great injustices make me sad.

They make me feel great pain and compassion for those who suffered terrible wrongs on our shores; however, black history also amazes me with the human ability to overcome.

"The Negro's past, this endless struggle to achieve and reveal a human identity, human authority; yet contains for all its horror, something very beautiful."–James Baldwin

6) When I read black history, I discover and am challenged by a passionate Christian faith and trust in God that is a rarity in our present time.

Black and White

To heal America's racial problems, we need to go back to the foundations of the problem. If race relations were built on a faulty foundation, while we purposefully ignore the details of that foundation, we would never be able to repair the black/white relationship in American society. Millions of black and white individuals have good relationships and get along; but in society at large, black and white race problems are still a major source of friction and pain.

Some people believe America's race problems are now solved. However, when unarmed black men are shot (or even mistreated) by the police, isn't that a societal problem? When millions of people feel they are second class citizens, isn't that a problem? When there are major disparities in income, imprisonment, poverty, education, etc., based on skin color, could that be considered a problem?

The historic enslavement and abuse of Africans and their descendants in America wasn't done by anyone currently alive or done to anyone currently alive. So, perhaps we can talk about it and search for the truth about it, objectively, rather than emotionally.

A Light Upon America's Colorful History of Slavery?

Slavery? "Forget it. It's over. It was dealt with by the Civil War. Don't dredge up the past. Let's move forward . . . there's nothing there, there." That's the opinion of many whites. For instance, when I told a white friend that I was writing a book about race, he said in an annoyed tone of voice: "Race! That's just identity politics!"

However, most Americans boldly remember the terrible acts done on American soil at Pearl Harbor and on 9/11. They say: "We will never forget!"

Slavery was also a terrible act. It lasted on American soil from 1619 to 1865 (almost 250 years). So, what's the difference?

Pearl Harbor and 9/11 were committed by non-Americans; but human enslavement was committed by a great many white Americans (including some who are considered to be our greatest heroes; even, Founding Fathers). It was also supported directly or indirectly by many white Americans and by the government. To memorialize slavery as a terrible thing, to clearly expose it's evil, and to honor the heroes who resisted it and fought it, would make our white forefathers look bad.

Perhaps it is time to overcome this great inconsistency. If we like to remember the truth about Pearl Harbor and call it "a day that will live in infamy;" if we will "never forget" 9/11; how can we say let's forget about slavery? Maybe we need to publicly remember the truth and the horrors of American slavery and let it be 250 years that will live in infamy?

How did Slavery Start in the USA?

In 1619, a Dutch human trafficker was trying to take a boatload of his African victims to the Spanish colonies in America. However, his boat was blown off course to the north and wound up eventually docking in Jamestown, Virginia after first landing at Point Comfort. (Prior to this time about 200,000 Africans had already been forcibly brought to non-British parts of the Americas as slaves.)

The Dutch ship captain sold his captives in Jamestown. A document written by John Rolfe, husband of Pocahontas and a Jamestown colonial official, gives a brief eye witness account. Rolfe wrote:

"He brought not anything but 20 and odd Negroes, which the Governor and Cape Merchant bought for victuals (whereof he was in great need as he portended) at the best and easiest rate they could."

These were the first Africans brought to territory

that would eventually become the United States. Notice that at this point, color-based racism had not been established in Jamestown. Skin color didn't seem to be an issue, at least not with John Rolfe. Although he was white, he was married to a Native American and his interracial marriage was accepted by the community. Rolfe also made no reference to the color of the new arrivals. He simple called them "Negroes." Also, the people of Jamestown didn't immediately make the new arrivals slaves; rather they made them indentured servants.

Indentured servants were normally Europeans who couldn't afford passage to the American colonies, so someone (or a company) would pay for their passage and they would work a set number of years until the person (or company) was paid back with profit. That was usually a seven-year period. (This was a common way for poor white people to move from England to America.) So, at the very beginning of black/white relationships in America, the first "20 and odd Negroes" were treated the same way poor Brits were treated. Some of those first blacks were set free at the end of their term and that was the beginning of the free black population in the Colonies.

There were several labor problems with white indentured servants. For one thing, they could run away and blend in with the general population. Second, their time of service was limited. Third, there were some laws and rules protecting them. And fourth, sometimes they had trouble getting enough indentured servants to meet their labor needs, especially for the extremely hard work with their tobacco crops.

However, because in the colonists considered blacks to be heather, savages who couldn't speak or read English when they were brought to the colonies, they soon felt free to go beyond having blacks as indentured servants and instead made them lifetime slaves with no legal rights or protections. Also, blacks couldn't just disappear into the general population, because their skin color made it obvious that they were runaway slaves. Besides that, the practice of African slavery in the Americas had already been established by Spain and other European nations; so why not the British colonists as well?

Definition of Blackness

Rather than lighting a candle for the Africans who were trafficked to the colonies, the American colonists cursed their darkness. Why?

Since almost all those early slaveholders in the colonies considered themselves to be Christians, they felt the need to justify their human trafficking and other abuses of blacks. Therefore, they basically defined blackness as a condition of being less than human and worthy of every kind of mistreatment and abuse, including being enslaved for life with absolutely no rights. They embraced and propagated the false idea that black Africans are not the same sort of beings as white Europeans—that blacks are somehow an inferior life form—a different race than whites. This made the Colonists' conscience (and their descendants' conscience, even until today) feel better about their doing terrible things to the blacks they claimed to own.

However, how does logic define blackness? Logically, blackness is a darker skin tone common to peoples from sub-Sahara Africa and to their descendants. That's all. Other definitions of blackness are emotive or rationalizations, but they aren't based on logic.

Ignoring logic, reason, and compassion, different colonial legislatures began to make laws taking away both the rights of blacks and their humanity. For example, in 1662, the Virginia General Assembly passed a law reversing the long-time, European precedent that a child's status is determined by its father. Thus, any children born to a white father and black mother would most likely be a slave (as determined by the black mother's status). The law read: "All children born in this country shall be held bond or free only according to the condition of the mother."

In 1664, the Maryland General Assembly enacted a law making slavery a legal institution and condemning all blacks to it for life. It read: "All Negroes or other slaves already within the province, and all Negroes and other slaves to be hereafter imported into the province, shall serve *durante vita* (for life). And all children born of any Negro or other slave shall be slaves as their fathers were for the term of their lives."

However, in the earliest days of colonial slavery,

there were a few courageous, white people who boldly spoke out against the false definition of blackness. One such person was Morgan Godwyn. He wrote that many people were holding the position "that the Negroes, though in their figure they carry some resemblances of manhood, yet are indeed no men." He refuted that idea as a "disingenuous and unmanly position." Godwyn called it "a fiction hardly to be parallel throughout the fables of the poets," based on "our planters' chief deity, profit."

Godwyn wrote: "Their limbs and members; their voice and countenance, in all things according with other men's; together with their risibility and discourse (man's peculiar faculties) should be sufficient conviction" of their full humanity. He goes on to say: "How should they otherwise be capable of trades, and other no less manly employments; as also of reading and writing; or show so much discretion in management of business, eminent in diverse of them; but wherein many of our own people are deficient; were they not truly men?"

Godwyn then asked a key question that perhaps we need to ask as we try to understand slavery. He asks: "Why should they be tormented and whipped almost (and sometimes quite) to death, upon any, whether small or great miscarriages?" He also refers to how slaveholders began twisting Scripture to try to back up their lie that blacks are inferior to whites. Godwyn then says; "From thence, as occasion shall offer, they'll infer their Negro's brutality (brutishness); justify their reduction of them under bondage; disable them from all right and claims."

He wrote that the justification of cruelty to and enslavement of Africans seems "to have been drawn from these four pretenses: the complexion, bondage, pretended stupidity; and barbarousness of our negro's manners, because different from ours." Talking about blackness, Godwyn wonders why "from so poor a medium (as skin color), our negro's brutality should be inferred." He says that in another part of the world, "they only may be the men and ourselves but beasts."

Another white voice against the false definition of blackness was Boston judge, Samuel Sewall. He wrote an anti-slavery pamphlet in 1700, calling slavery "the most atrocious of capital crimes." Sewall wrote: "The numerousness of slaves at this day in the province, and the uneasiness of them under their slavery, hath put many upon thinking whether the foundation of it be firmly and well laid."

Because black and white relations were built on such an unjust foundation, we need to confront and challenge that false foundation today. This was not a little white lie about black men, women, and children. As we have seen, the lie says that black skin is somehow shameful. That big lie, buried deep within our national subconsciousness, releases negative, emotional reactions (uneasiness, suspicion, caution, dislike, fear, disdain, superiority, anger, etc.) when a great many Americans see black skin. (And sometimes, even when blacks see their own skin.) Then those reactions often make us blind to the unique person within black skin. That's why, to ever have really good black/white relations, our society must overcome the lie. Perhaps, Sewall's 1700 pamphlet can teach us something to help us in the Twenty-First Century.

Sewell went contrary to the popular opinion of his day and courageously wrote: "It is most certain that all men, as they are sons of Adam, are and have equal right unto liberty. God has made of one blood all nations of men." (Unlike the U.S. Declaration of Independence, Sewell really did mean *all men* including blacks.)

Like an Old Testament prophet, Sewell proclaimed: "Seeing God has said, he that steals a man and sells him, or if he be found in his hand, he shall surely be put to death. Exodus 12:16. This Law being of Everlasting Equity, wherein man stealing is ranked among the most atrocious of capital crimes. What louder cry can there be made of the celebrated warning. Caveat Emptor!" It's one of history's greatest tragedies that the colonists and later the Americans ignored Sewell's warning.

Sewell added: "How horrible is the uncleanness, mortality, if not murder, that the ships are guilty of that bring great crowds of these miserable men and women." He then gives four reasons the colonists used to justify the human trafficking and enslavement of blacks.

First, he refers to the so-called *Curse of Ham* in the Bible. I'll explain more about this falsehood at the end of this section.

Second, he says people say blacks are "brought out of a pagan country, into places where the Gospel is preached." He answers this obtuse justification by saying: "Evil must not be done that good may come of it."

Third, Sewell, says people try to justify slavery by saying "the Africans have wars with one another: our ships bring lawful captives taken in those wars." He refutes it with: "Every war is upon one side unjust. An unlawful war can't make lawful captives. And by receiving, we are in danger to promote, and partake in their barbarous cruelties. (That was definitely prophetic. The barbarous cruelties of 250 years of American slavery and 90 years of forced, legal segregation can never be overstated.)

Fourth, he quotes the justifiers of abusing blacks as saying: "Abraham had servants bought with his money and born in his house." Sewell responds: "Our Blessed Savior has altered the measures of the ancient love-song and set it to a most excellent new tune, which all ought to be ambitious of learning."

Sewell concludes with this statement: "These Ethiopians, as black as they are; seeing they are the sons and daughters of the first Adam, the brethren and sisters of the last ADAM, and the offspring of God; they ought to be treated with respect."

Sewell and Godwyn were ignored in their day. But shouldn't they be heard in ours? Isn't it time to respect black Americans enough to bring to light the details of the terrible things done to them by our white American forefathers? Isn't it time to refute and to renounce the terrible lie of inferiority that has devalued American blacks since the 1600s? "Oh," you say, "I wasn't there for these racial inequities and horrid atrocities—how can I be held accountable?" My friend, as an American, as a human being, you, nor I, nor any of us, can gloss over our heritage without revealing the awfulness of its past injustices, lest we repeat her glaring infractions in the name of ignorance to crimes committed. It is not sufficient to give a nod to history's promiscuous past—rather to expose and renounce its miserable inequities should be our posture!

Today's Definition of Blackness

Which definition of blackness does white America hold in the Twenty-First Century—the logical one or the lie? If we boldly refute and renounce the big lie and we clearly and openly redefine blackness as being nothing more than skin color, then we have a problem. In that case our forefathers were guilty of human trafficking, running concentration camps called plantations, abuse, torture, rape, child abuse of their own children held in slavery, and other crimes against humanity. It means there was something terribly wrong with our forefathers' morals, mental health, beliefs and behaviors.

However, if we can somehow believe there is something inherent within blackness which justifies our forefathers' centuries' long abuse of blacks, then we can protect our cherished ideas of their greatness. Therein lies the rub, the dilemma, which many of us whites unconsciously hold as a distorted belief. That belief is: For so many great Americans to have treated blacks so cruelly, and for our nation to boast in freedom, and then to have supported the owning and trafficking of blacks as nothing more than chattel, there must be something in blacks that deserved it, because our freedom-loving forefathers couldn't have committed such unjustified crimes against humanity.

To fully embrace the truth that blacks are and have always been fully human, casts many of our white American forefathers as perpetrators of some of the worst crimes in human history. Yes, that is very painful to hear and to admit, for we are wont to hold on to denial. Thus, we try (often unconsciously) to hold two contradictory beliefs at the same time. Our American forefathers were good people and so are African-Americans. If that's the case, how incongruous: American history shows good people doing horrible things to good people.

Gradually, the concept of race and color-inferiority in America was expanded beyond black and white. In addition to being used to justify African-American slavery, it was also used to justify the taking of Indian and Mexican land and the exclusion of and mistreatment of Asian immigrants—while wholly justified by the peculiar notion of MANIFEST DESTINY (i.e., God deigned it to be so!). In the Twentieth Century race was used to justify the taking over of foreign nations and lands, such as the Philippines, Hawaii, and Puerto Rico.

I am so grateful that slavery and legalized color segregation are gone. However, perhaps the biggest racial problem in American is the mythical definition of blacks as different from and in some ways inferior to whites. This remains in various degrees. As a child I suffered from great feelings of inferiority because of my lack of sports ability. Similarly, no one should ever have those self-inflicting feelings of inferiority put on them because of their skin color. No one!

Curse of Ham?

Slaveholder propaganda is still circulating in America in the Twenty-First Century, even in the black community. Here are three examples:

1) A few years ago, a black man I had never met stopped his beautiful, red pick-up truck beside me as I was standing on Natchez Street in Franklin, Tennessee. Almost the first thing he said to me was, "You know, we black people are under a curse." "What?" I asked. "Oh yeah," he said. "God cursed us in the Bible." This guy looked prosperous and was very intelligent and articulate. And yet he debated with me (a white guy) for twenty minutes, that blacks were cursed by God in the Bible.

2) A white church I formerly attended once had a Somali guest preacher and choir. The first thing this African man said when he stood to preach was something like this: "You know, we black people are under God's curse."

3) A prominent black preacher, who is a friend of mine, gave me a copy of a book he wrote. In

that book he repeatedly states all black people have a biblical curse on them.

Where did those black people get the idea blacks are cursed? It is nothing more than slaveholder propaganda. As we have seen, white people felt compelled to justify their wicked behavior toward blacks and often turned to the Bible looking for some justification. By distorting and twisting Genesis chapter 9, verses 20-27, they developed the so-called *Curse of Ham*.

Slave holders proclaimed the descendants of Ham (a son of Noah) were the Africans—they all shared in a curse and were supposed to be enslaved by other races. Let's set the record straight! In his book, *The Black Man—Cursed or Blessed?"* Church of God In Christ author, Scott A. Bradley, says:

"I began to read these scriptures in Genesis Chapter 9 and through much prayer and study I find that there is no such curse of races as we have been told for centuries."

If you read this passage you will see that Noah got drunk one day and was physically exposed in his tent. One of his sons, Ham, came in and "saw the nakedness of his father," and told his two brothers. The brothers, Shem and Japheth, backed into Noah's tent and covered his nakedness. When Noah came to from his drunkenness he realized "what his younger son had done unto him."
Then Noah said: "Cursed be Canaan, a servant of servants shall he be unto his brethren." Please notice that a hung-over Noah spoke this "curse" and

not God. Also note that the "curse" was on an individual named Canaan (Ham's youngest son), and not on Ham nor on any of Ham's descendants besides his youngest son, Canaan. Bradly points out that "Noah did not have three races of sons." Indeed, there is absolutely no mention of race or color or black people in this passage, yet it was used for 250 years as an attempt to biblically justify the enslavement of Africans.

No one knows for sure, who today are Ham's descendants. But whoever they are, they are not cursed. The best explanation I have ever found for this passage is that after Noah woke up from his drunkenness, he realized that Ham had molested him. Then when he said: "Cursed be Canaan," he was describing Canaan's situation of having a father who is a molester, not personally cursing him. (Notice he did not say, "I curse Canaan," but instead stated Canaan was cursed.)

If Noah had wanted to speak a curse on someone, wouldn't he have cursed Ham, the person who did the act, rather than the innocent son? Canaan was probably still a child and would be living with a father who was a molester. Now that is a cursed situation for any child.

This passage in no way either states or implies that God put a curse on black people! How can it be so? It never mentions color! A hung-over Noah, not God, is the one who says "cursed." The statement is directed at one person only, Canaan, and not toward any group or race of people!

Another interpretation posits the notion that Canaan, being cursed, later had 11 sons himself. These 11 sons are antithetical to the 12 sons of Jacob/Israel. They initially settled in the "Land of Canaan" and were known as the Canaanites (a Mediterranean race of people—hardly black). The Lord brought the Children of Israel into the land of the Canaanites because the "Iniquity of the Amorites was full." They had to be expunged from the land because their iniquities had "reached to the heavens." Therefore, God brought the Israelite slaves out of Egypt to inherit the Good Land.

However, this said, the list of Shem, Ham, and Japheth's descendants which follows this chapter in the Bible, never mentions either race or a curse on a particular group of Noah's descendants. Bradley says: "From the sons of Noah came the table of nations, not the table of races as some believe."

Conclusion: The "curse of Ham being on black people" is a complete and total falsehood.

It is sad this falsehood regarding the *Curse of Ham* still lingers in America. Yet it was officially preached by the church and officially taught by the government from 1619 onward when the first black slaves arrived, until the 1960s when church and state both took away their official support of this falsehood. After 350 years of propaganda, it is not easily expunged from our "biblical lexicons."

I encourage you to examine this passage of Scripture for yourself. Set aside what you have been taught and read it as it is. Does it say: "God cursed black people?" Be honest. Then read "John 3:16."

There you will see that God so loved the world (the people, not the real estate) that He gave Jesus for us all! Red and yellow, black and white, ALL are precious in His sight!

Civil War Between the States

America had a big war—brother against brother—that began in 1861. They called it *civil,* but it was not. Hundreds of thousands of Americans were slaughtered by battle and disease. The physical devastation was tremendous—billions of dollars spent on warfare led to burned homes, pillaged countryside, huge losses in crops and farm animals, ruined bridges, buildings, and roads.

In our day it is popular to reenact the horror of America's big war. Several hundred thousand Americans regularly dress up in Blue or Gray uniforms pretending they are reliving all that destruction. What are they reenacting?

President Abraham Lincoln came to believe that the big war was God's judgment on America for the sin of slavery. In his Second Inaugural Address Lincoln said:

> "If God wills that it (the big war) continue until all the wealth piled up by the bondsman's two hundred and fifty years of unrequited toil shall be sunk, and until every drop of blood drawn by the lash shall be paid by another drawn with the sword, as was said three thousand years ago, so still must it be said, 'The judgments of the Lord are true and righteous altogether.'"

Ellen G. White, a founder of the Seventh Day Adventist denomination said during the big war:

> "God is punishing this nation for the high crime of slavery. He will punish the South for the sin of slavery and the North for so long allowing its overreaching and overbearing influence."

William Lloyd Garrison said:

> "I have never been an enemy of the South, and in the desire to save her from this great retribution (the big war) I demanded in the name of the living God that every fetter should be broken and the oppressed set free."

The Union soldiers acknowledged God's judgment as they sang:

> "He is sifting out the hearts of men before His judgment seat."

W.E.B. DuBois said:

> "The Negro knew full well that whatever their deeper convictions may have been, Southern men had fought with desperate energy to perpetuate the slavery under which the black masses shivered."

United States Senator, Charles Sumner, said on June 4, 1860.

> "Look at slavery in the light of principles and it is

nothing less than a huge insurrection against the eternal law of God."

Southern blacks also saw the big war as God's judgment on slavery. Harper's Weekly published "The Freedman's Song" in 1865 which said:

> "The Lord, He made us free indeed, In His own time and way."

Rev. E.K. Love said in 1891:

> "Emancipation Day marks the day when the mighty arm of Jehovah was moved in our defense and effected eternally our deliverance."

Southerners in The Union Army

Almost 200,000 Southerners fought for the Union army. These were people born and bred in the South, whose families went back for generations. They felt they had been mistreated by their fellow Southerners and sided with the Union because they and their families had, over a period of 250 years, been held in life-long bondage. For those Southerners the big war was not about "states rights to enslave them" but about their personal right to "life, liberty, and the pursuit of happiness."

Samuel Allen McElwee, a black Tennessean, spoke to the state legislature on February 23, 1887 and said:

> "For years American slavery was the great sin of the nation. In the course of time God made clear

His disapproval of this national sin by a national calamity. Four years of destruction and bloody war rent our country in twain and left our Southland devastated. The war came as a result of sin; let us sin no more lest a greater calamity befall us."

As Americans in our day casually reenact God's powerful judgment on America, it is important to ask: Has the root of the sin of slavery (the false definition of blackness) that brought this judgment, been removed from America? Have the lies that were used to justify slavery—color prejudice, black inferiority, social inequality, the *Curse of Ham*, segregation—been once and for all put away? The Civil War ended official slavery in America, but did it bring true freedom to blacks?

What About After Slavery?

Immediately, after slavery was ended in America, blacks had great hope. They had been set free—emancipated! It was their moment of jubilee.

Blacks left plantations in droves, often searching for family members who had been separated by selling. However, some blacks stayed behind because they didn't know any other life. Others stayed because they felt a sense of loyalty to their former masters. All their lives as slaves, they had been told what to do and punished if they didn't do it. Almost none had been allowed to learn to read; in fact, they were severely punished if they tried. Most had few marketable skills beyond those that involved hard farm labor. As hostile as the environment had been on their plantation, many former slaves were afraid it could be even more hostile if they left.

The time period from 1866 to 1877 was called Reconstruction. During this time, Northern troops were still in Southern States. Reconstruction was implemented by the U.S. Congress, in order to reorganize the Southern states after the Civil War, and to provide the means for readmitting them into the Union, and to establish ways that blacks and whites could live together in a society without slavery.

During Reconstruction, black and white teachers, churches, missionary organizations, and schools worked energetically to give the freed slaves, known as Freedmen, the chance to learn. Many of the Southern black colleges were founded during that period.

With the passing of the Thirteenth, Fourteenth, and Fifteenth Amendments to the Constitution and the Civil Rights Act of 1866, African Americans enjoyed a short time in which they finally had the opportunity to work for themselves and improve their own lives. Many Southern blacks began to improve their condition and to prosper. Individual blacks learned how to read, start businesses, acquire new skills, acquire property, reassembled their families split up by slavery, built houses, got jobs, began to use public accommodations, and got involved in Southern politics by voting and getting elected to office.

During Reconstruction about 2,000 blacks were elected to public office across the South. That included a U.S. Senator, 16 U. S. Congressmen, and more than 600 elected to state legislatures.

However, there was much animosity to the improvement of blacks. Much of the white population resisted the newly freed people and began to find ways for stopping and reversing black progress. After the final federal troops were pulled out of the South in 1877, whites became much bolder.

The Southern white effort to reestablish control over the black population was called *Disenfranchisement*. Whites rallied against the new U.S. Constitutional Amendments that had ended slavery, made blacks official American citizens, and given black men the right to vote. They began to pass laws and change state constitutions to negate federal laws which guaranteed blacks equal rights. Southern whites especially targeted the right to vote and eventually disenfranchised the vast majority of blacks from voting.

The white Southerners who led this effort were called the *Redeemers*. Their goal was to destroy the free interaction between blacks, whites, and the political institutions which had been formed during Reconstruction. They wanted to separate blacks from whites and to reassert white rule in and control of the South—they gradually succeeded. In addition to political means, they also used violence while establishing terrorist organizations to intimidate and force blacks into submission.

This led to the *Jim Crow* period of American history. "***Jim Crow***" was a derogatory slang word for a black man. It began to be applied to any state law passed in the South that created different rules for blacks and whites. Those laws were based on keeping whites in control and were a reaction to Reconstruction.

By the 1890s a depression was sweeping the country; whites were afraid of losing jobs to blacks. So white politicians in Southern states began to pass laws to protect whites and their "rights." Eventually Jim Crow laws mandated racial segregation in all public facilities in all the states of the former Confederacy.

Blacks were supposedly given "separate but equal status."

In 1890, despite still having 16 black members, the Louisiana General Assembly made it illegal for black and white people to ride together on railroads. Then in 1896, the U.S. Supreme Court, made up of all white men, heard Homer Plessy's story about being forbidden to ride in the "whites only" section of a train coach by that state law of Louisiana. If Homer, a Louisianan of mixed race, wanted to ride, the state law said he had to ride in a coach set aside for black people.

Homer Plessy insisted enforced segregation compromised the principle of legal equality and marked blacks as inferior. All the Supreme Court Justices, except one, voted forced segregation was constitutional. The majority justices wrote:

"If one race be inferior to the other socially, the

Constitution of the United States cannot put them upon the same place."

This judgment legally separated America's blacks and whites. It basically canceled the Fourteenth Amendment to the Constitution, which says: "No state shall make or enforce any law which shall abridge the privileges or immunities of citizens of the United States." Those justices cleared the way for legally sanctioned racism, intimidation, discrimination, segregation, terrorism, persecution, and lynching of black people for the next sixty years. For example, at the time of this ruling, in 1896, more than 130,000 African-Americans in Louisiana were registered to vote. Ten years later there were only about 1,300. One lone white man on the Supreme Court, however, said NO – Justice John Marshall Harlan. He wrote:

> "In the eyes of the law, there is in this country no ruling class of citizens. There is no caste here. Our constitution is colorblind, and neither knows nor tolerates classes among citizens. In respect of civil rights, all citizens are equal before the law. The humblest is the peer of the most powerful. The arbitrary separation of citizens on the basis of race, while they are on a public highway, is a badge of servitude wholly inconsistent with the civil freedom and the equality before the law established by the Constitution. It cannot be justified upon any legal grounds."

Who was John Harlan, this hero who dared to speak the truth against American racism in the highest court in the land? John Harlan of Kentucky, was a former slave-holder and defender of slavery. He had fought for the Union Army but had spoken against the Emancipation Proclamation (which did not apply to Kentucky). John Harlan did not free his slaves until the ratification of the Thirteenth Amendment forced him to in December 1865.

Six years later, in 1871, Harlan, former slave-holder, said:

> "I have lived long enough to feel and declare that the most perfect despotism that ever existed on this earth was the institution of African slavery. With slavery it was death or tribute. It knew no compromise, it tolerated no middle course. I rejoice that it is gone."

When asked about his about face regarding the issue of slavery, John Harlan would reply:

> "Let it be said that I am right rather than consistent."

What could have changed him so? Something must have touched his heart.

The terrorism of the Ku Klux Klan in Kentucky pushed him toward equal rights. He was shocked by the arson, beatings, and murders. He became friends with a leading Republican, Benjamin Bristow, who was the United States Attorney for Kentucky. Bristow fearlessly prosecuted the white terrorists. Somehow Harlan saw the truth of the wickedness of American racial injustice, and when he did, he never looked back.

That is why John Harlan could stand alone in 1896 and boldly say:

> "In my opinion, the judgment this day rendered will, in time, prove to be quite as pernicious as the decision made by this tribunal in the Dred Scott Case."

Like a prophet, John said:

> "The thin disguise of *equal* accommodations will not mislead anyone, nor atone for the wrong this day done."

Two years later, the Supreme Court upheld a Mississippi law designed to deny black men the vote. Southern states saw this as a green light to pass even more laws stripping black people of their legal rights and of legal protection and keeping them under white domination and control. This resulted in a long period of total, strict, and forcibly enforced segregation lasting until the Civil Rights Movement beginning in the 1950s.

Civil Rights Movement

More than 360,000 blacks served in a segregated American army during World War I. They were welcomed home with 25 major race riots. White mobs even lynched some veterans in uniform.

In World War II the U.S. Armed forces were still segregated. Although blacks served heroically, after the war they still weren't given equal rights. This helped lead to the Civil Rights Movement, which was an organized effort by blacks in America to end racial discrimination and segregation to gain equal rights under the law. It lasted from the late 1940s until the early 1970s. The movement, although mostly nonviolent, drew violent responses from many whites.

However, the end result was laws passed to protect every American's constitutional rights, in spite of color, race, sex or national origin.

Freedom Riders of The Civil Rights Movement

I watched a two-hour documentary on PBS about the Freedom Riders, a group of young people (mostly college students) both black and white (committed to non-violence), who rode public buses together into the Deep South (in 1961) to challenge state segregation laws ruled unconstitutional by the US Supreme Court. Watching the courage, commitment, and heroism of the Freedom Riders was deeply moving.

The first group left on two buses from Washington DC with the intention of riding all the way to New Orleans. In Anniston, Alabama, the first bus was surrounded by an angry white mob. The mob broke out a window, threw a fire bomb inside, and held the door shut. Finally, someone in the mob yelled out the bus was going to explode. The mob ran away, allowing the choking Freedom Riders to get out of the bus just in time. As they lay on the ground, a courageous, color-kind white girl, ignored the mob and brought them water.

The second bus arrived in Birmingham, unaware of what had happened to the people on the first bus. As they entered the bus terminal, it was filled with hate-filled whites who began to beat them with bats and crow bars while kicking them. (The local police had promised the mob 15 minutes to do whatever they wanted to the Freedom Riders.) Then the riders from both buses were put in the Birmingham jail. Eventually, with the help of the federal government, they were extracted from Alabama on a plane.

At that time, a group of Fisk University students in Nashville, felt like the Freedom Rides should not be ended because of violence. So, they decided to ride a bus as a mixed group of blacks and whites the next day. They were going to Birmingham and then on to New Orleans.

John Seigenthaler, who was US Attorney General, Robert Kennedy's assistant, had been dispatched to Birmingham to try to help protect the Freedom Riders. He called the leader of the Fisk Freedom Riders, Diane Nash, and told her not to come to Birmingham. She told him they were coming, no matter what. He said something like: "You don't understand, the situation is so bad that somebody is going to get killed." She replied: "You don't understand, we signed our last will and testament last night."

The Fisk Freedom Riders made it to Birmingham and were allowed to go on to Jackson, Mississippi. There they were arrested and put in the worst prison in Mississippi. Then another group of Fisk students left for Jackson. They too were put in the same prison. Eventually more than 400 Freedom Riders, both blacks and whites, were put in that notorious prison.

Finally, the federal government required states to end segregation on all buses and in all bus terminals involved in interstate commerce. The courageous non-violence of the Freedom Riders won a great victory for freedom in America and helped the Civil Rights Movement grow stronger and bolder.

Watching the documentary, I kept thinking about how we need people like the Freedom Riders today, especially in the church. Nowadays, churches are perhaps the most segregated groups in America, when according to the Bible, they should look like Heaven and should be the most multicultural and multiethnic groups in the country. I prayed: "Lord, raise up people like the Freedom Riders, who will risk all to cross racial lines and bring racial reconciliation to Your church."

Then the next day, I was encouraged to attend a class on leadership at Trevecca Nazarene University. When I arrived, the class turned out to be about how to make a church multi-racial and multicultural, rather than about leadership in general. The class was based on the biblical idea church should have the diversity of Heaven, people from "every kindred and every tribe."

The class reminded me of when I first saw the movie, *Return of the Titans* (about the integration of a Southern high school football team). Watching that movie, I was moved to tears and I kept asking God; "Lord, let me help bring the church together across racial lines the way that coach brought that team, school, and town together across racial lines."

Perhaps it is time for some courageous Freedom Worshippers to leave their mostly white, black, or cultural church, and go to be part of a church of another race or ethnicity.

Monteagle, Tennessee Civil Rights Movement

Here is a little-known fact of American history. Monteagle, Tennessee could be called the cradle of the Civil Rights Movement. Before the Civil Rights Movement began, Martin Luther King, Jr., Ralph Abernathy, Rosa Parks and many other future leaders of the Movement were trained in non-violent action at Highlander Folk School in Monteagle, Tennessee. The school was founded and led by Myles Horton, a white Tennessean. The main instructor was an African American woman, Septima Poinsette Clark.

Horton suffered much persecution for his bold stand for liberty and justice for all, in the days of Jim Crow racism in Tennessee. In 1960 his school, home, and land were seized by the State of Tennessee and he was forced to move out of Monteagle.

I first learned about Horton a few years ago when a street in Nashville was named for Rosa Parks. Someone wrote a column in *The Tennessean* and said that a street should also be named for the

Tennessean who helped train Rosa Parks, Myles Horton. I was moved to hear about such a color-kind, American hero who was hated by many in his day and is almost unknown nowadays.

Once my wife and I were driving to Chattanooga from Nashville. We stopped in Monteagle to have lunch with some friends. I was thinking I wish I could find the building where Highlander Folk School had been located. I had been in Monteagle several times but had never found anyone who knew anything about it. We were about an hour early for lunch, so we decided to drive around a campground called the Monteagle Assembly. Before we went through the gate, I felt led to ask the woman working there if she knew where Highlander Folk School had been located. She said: "I live right across the road from it." Then she gave us directions.

As we drove down a one lane country road we finally saw a sign that read "Old Highlander Road." We turned left and then we found the building, now a private residence, where First Lady Eleanor Roosevelt once spoke, where Pete Seeger sang, and where many of America's great Civil Rights leaders were trained.

There is nothing to mark this spot in Tennessee that was so influential in bringing about a freer America. However, the vision, the humility, and the greatness that came together there, although mainly unknown or forgotten, rang in my heart as I a saw the building so critical to a movement. I felt I was in a sanctuary of freedom.

Selma

Seeing the movie, *Selma*, stirred my soul! It made me weep. When I saw it, it received an ongoing standing ovation from a theater packed with both blacks and whites in Nashville!

Selma strikingly portrays a major turning point in the Civil Rights Movement during a three-month period in 1965, when Dr. Martin Luther King, Jr. courageously led a campaign, in the face of violent opposition in Selma, Alabama, seeking equal voting rights for all. Against all odds, Dr. King successfully led a march from Selma to Montgomery, resulting in the Voting Rights Act of 1965, signed by President Lyndon Johnson.

Director Ava DuVernays beautifully portrays the stirring story of Selma. He shows how King (David Oyelowo) and other people inspired by their faith, both blacks and whites, united in the Movement and prompted change that overthrew much of America's overt and legal racism.

> "One dream can change the world!" *Selma* makes it clear it was King's dream, calling, and courage which came from God. The film is full of Gospel Music, Bible verses, and praying in public. At one point, when King is struggling with obedience to his calling, he phones famous Gospel singer, Mahalia Jackson, and asks her to sing a spiritual song to him. Throughout the film, King is shown preaching. Many scenes are set in church services. King's dream deeply touches my heart's desire to see racial injustice and hurt completely

healed in America. As police shootings of unarmed black men has shown us, we've still got a mountain top to climb!

Stages of Racism in America

American racism against African-Americans has evolved through three stages:

1) Slavery: Forcefully abusing blacks by human trafficking them as property;

2) Segregation: Actively rejecting blacks, openly insulting them, and forcefully keeping them separated from whites; and . . .

3) Colorblindness: Ignoring blacks and the institutional problems they face.

Perhaps it is time to move into a fourth stage which goes beyond both active racism and passive avoidance. Perhaps it's time to go beyond colorblindness to *color-kindness*, beyond color-avoidance to *color-appreciation*.

6. *Skin Colors—Plantations—Chattanooga*

Creative Skin Color Concepts, 3 Nashville Plantation Visits in 3 Days, and a Trip to Chattanooga

Original Skin Color Thoughts

The color of the skin you live in gives no indication of the kind of person you have been. Skin shade is a thin disguise hiding who you really are. However, despite that, some people are so *creativity challenged* they find the only reason they can think of not to like someone is the color of their skin.

It's strange how skin color can cause a distinctive person within the skin to be invisible to some people. Racial profiling is fear-sighted people seeing suspicion and danger in a particular skin color.

Skin coloration is like wrapping paper, decorating the amazing gift of a human friend. Look beyond the color and unwrap the gift of someone who is shaded differently than you are.

To appreciate skin color takes openness and commitment; not a miracle. Some people are so thick skinned they are unwilling to appreciate anybody's skin color but their own.

To get hung up about the shade of person's skin creates a lot of *surface tension* in society. A terrible skin disease is to be at *dis-ease* with the coloration of human skin.

How can there be only three races based on skin color when there are more than fifty shades of skin? The concept of race has run out of gas. Instead of bottling and selling racism, early Americans enslaved and sold the victims of their racism. Their skin chauvinism is a worn-out idea still leaving in its wake hate and destruction contaminating the world. A culture that creates and cultivates color-self-consciousness contains unresolved conflicts, bitterness, resentment and chaos.

Early in American history, black skin was branded as substandard. Because most of the details of that branding are now hidden outside of our historical consciousness, we now find Americans still have trouble getting beyond the blackness-brand and getting it out of their hearts and minds. However, to look down on darker skin color poisons the soul.

It's time to move beyond racial myths to warmly embrace the race of many colors—humanity! So, let's race some laps around American history and try to erase some of the racial confusion. Even though American history tried to make us all a part of a race on a color-coded track, we now need to learn how to let all of us colorful people (regardless of our shade) embrace our corporate race—humankind!

Imagine human skin color being an inspiring gift from God instead of being seen as an object of hate. Prejudice is a form of blindness and no one likes to admit they are mentally blind.

When people are labeled by color they are denied the right to be seen by the individual responsibility of their own choices. The only people who are responsible for their skin color are those who intentionally soak up the sun or slip into tanning booths.

A color-based culture loses its bearings and creates much friction as it rolls along. Instead of skin-suspicion, let's embrace skin care and show kindness to people who look different than us. What skin color is your soul?

It's time for some common sense thinking about skin color. Let's begin with: The skin you live in doesn't change the kind of person you are. There is no such thing as "bad skin color." If you have skin to live in, it's a blessing, regardless of the coloration.

Too bad we can't walk awhile in each other's skin. Even if we could, would we be willing to do so? Genuine racial reconciliation requires racial justice that requires honestly looking at and openly exposing the wrongs of the past, because, after all, past wrongs are the roots and foundations of today's injustices.

I wonder why you never hear anybody say; "Gimmie some skin perspective and wisdom so I can treat people better." (In fact, I've never said that. There, I just did!)

As I was writing this section, expressing my creativity, Ernie suggested we go tour Belle Meade

Mansion, a place in Nashville we have never toured, although we've lived here almost three decades. Someone had given her free tickets, so we went.

Belle Meade Plantation

Belle Meade was a 5,400-acre plantation, one of the largest in Nashville. In 1953 the mansion and the remaining 30 acres were bought by the Association for the Preservation of Tennessee Antiquities. It was restored and turned into a museum with event space.

As we toured the amazing mansion and grounds the tour guide told us there once were 136 slaves on the plantation. He didn't say much about the slaves or how they were treated, however, he did tell us we could go visit an exhibit in a slave house on the property. We did.

A display on the slave cabin wall said "unrealistic stereotypes . . . depicted the Southern slave as the 'happy-go-lucky' singing and dancing simpleton who lived in a paradise. Many Southern slave owners would force their slaves to sing, dance, and perform as proof they fit the characteristics of Minstrel characters and plots. Of course, the penalty for not performing varied from plantation to plantation, but violence was an ever-present option."

It went on to say:

> "Sadly, the Minstrel stereotype would remain entrenched in American popular culture

throughout the first half of the twentieth century in movies, cartoons, marketing, and jargon . . . It would take many years to overcome the Jim Crow stereotype."

Here's more from the wall of that slave cabin:

"Since the beginning of the transatlantic slave trade, Africans from different countries, cultures, languages, and creeds underwent a unifying transformation aboard slave vessels bound for the new world. In the eyes of their white captors, the men, women, and children of West Africa were unified in their skin color and now in their status as human cargo. Regardless of their background each newly enslaved human being was now considered a *black* human being and this racial label would serve as the catch-all ethnicity for all Africans and their artistic expressions for centuries to come . . . (which) were considered primitive, low class, uncultured, and *black* . . . and established the archetype of what it meant to be black in the eyes of white America."

I just found an article with this quote from Jenny Lamb, a historian at Belle Meade Plantation:

"For a long time, Belle Meade Plantation was a tour of a lovely home that was restored to post-Antebellum days, and a property that was popular for weddings and fancy events. Certain pieces of the history were not spoken of or were glossed over."

Ignoring or glossing over (and even justifying) the painful parts of American history has been (and still is) very common. I'm glad Belle Meade Plantation is beginning to share some details of what it was like to be an American slave.

John Lamb, a curator at Belle Meade put it this way:

> "In the past people may have been concerned about upsetting people or making them uncomfortable. It is upsetting and uncomfortable, to say the least. But it is an egregious (shocking and horrific) error not to tell it."

Here's another story I found in that slave house showing how American slavery was not only a terribly cruel and unjust institution, but how people sometimes went outside the system to be even more cruel. It's about how Susanna McGavock Carter was illegally made a slave at Belle Meade.

She was the daughter of a white Englishman and a mother who was part American Indian, part African-American. However, Susanna was born free. When her father passed away, her custody and that of her sisters was illegally transferred to Randal McGavock, who illegally made them slaves on his Carnton Plantation in Franklin. Tennessee.

Jenny Lamb continues the rest of the story:

> "Overnight, she went from being free to being a slave. When McGavock's daughter Elizabeth married John Harding's (owner of Belle Meade

Plantation) son, William Giles Harding, in 1840, Susanna was separated from her older sisters and brought as a slave to Belle Meade as part of Elizabeth's dowry. Susanna grew up enslaved on the plantation and married another slave named Isaac Carter, a stonemason. They had children here who were born into slavery."

So, two early Nashville area leaders (who both have streets named in their honor today), Randal McGavock and William Giles Harding, illegally enslaved Susanna and then illegally trafficked her from one plantation to another. However, another one of Harding's slaves went the other direction.

Ben, the blacksmith at Belle Meade (who had no known last name), was born into slavery in 1774 and was trafficked to Harding in 1806. In 1818, he claimed his human right as a man created equal and ran away. Harding placed an ad in the local paper offering $20.00 for his return, however, Ben was never found.

Hopefully, Ben was able to say, "Free at last, free at last . . . thank God Almighty, I'm free at last!"

Travellers Rest Plantation

Ernie had also been given tickets for a guided tour of Travellers Rest Plantation which is only about 12 blocks from our house. We had been to a wedding on the grounds once before but had never been in the mansion or on the guided tour. So, we went the day after we visited Belle Meade Plantation.

The first thing our guide told us as we were walking up to the house which was built in 1799 was the rise of the house was built on a Native American burial mound. She told us when the foundation was being dug, they found at least thirty sets of human remains and quickly added, "but nobody knows what they did with them." I was shocked! If someone would find a cemetery on their construction site how could they casually unearth the remains and continue building.

The guide told us that Judge John Overton, who owned Travelers Rest and is considered one of the great men in Tennessee history, was the lifelong best friend of President Andrew Jackson. Overton originally called his home Golgotha.

As we were touring the mansion, hearing the history of John Overton's life, and observing his lifestyle and possessions appearing so refined and cultured, I couldn't stop thinking all that was built on the graves of Native Americans and by the forced, unpaid labor of African-Americans. I kept wondering, how can this man be considered great when he knowingly desecrated graves and openly engaged in human trafficking so that he could have a lavish and affluent lifestyle. He was one of the richest men in Tennessee at the time.

Another interesting thing the guide told us was Overton was single until his early 50s. That also got me thinking, what heterosexual man (especially a single one) could own women as his personal property and not have sex with them? So, when I got home I searched the web for slave children of

John Overton. I found sites saying he had two famous African-American descendants. (To be much fairer to John than he was to the Native Americans whose graves he had his slaves build his house on, or to the people he enslaved, I'm not sure if John had children and made them his slaves, or if John's son, who took over the Plantation and slaves after him, had children and enslaved them, or both, or neither.)

Several web sites state Thomas "Hollywood" Henderson, a former NFL linebacker for the Dallas Cowboys, Houston Oilers, and Miami Dolphins and Richard Arvin Overton are both descendants of John Overton. Richard Arvin Overton (at this writing) is the oldest living American World War II veteran who just turned 112 in May of 2018.

Also, this advertisement was in the slave exhibit at Travellers Rest:

> "RUNAWAY My Negro man Harry, in the month of May last, a blacksmith owned by me for 30 years, and for the first time this last spring set up a claim for freedom under the name James Farmer, which is not believed by any person who knows him, as he was habitually regardless of truth when I bought him & he has continued so ever since. He is about 50 years of age, a large square built man, with a flat face, rather dour look, talks fast with facility and plausibility when he does talk . . . It is probable he may have a horse—as I understand that he has shewn papers certifying his freedom, which some wicked person must have forged for him. Whoever will

lodge said fellow in any jail, giving me information thereof by mail or otherwise shall receive $10 reward, and if delivered to me at home, 5 miles south of Nashville, $25 reward. July 18, 1828 JNO Overton."

It's interesting to note Judge Overton whose trial judgments set many legal precedents for the state of Tennessee, believed someone who helped a runaway slave keep his courageously acquired freedom, was "some wicked person."

Andrew Jackson's Hermitage & Slave Life

When most Americans think about life on a plantation, they think of the whites who lived there. Because American plantations weren't free or democratic institutions, most of the people's plantation experience was suppressed. They were not allowed to tell outsiders about their life on the plantation, under threat of violence. Being forced into secrecy, they had to risk their life to tell the majority story of plantation life (slavery).

Even today, if you visit a plantation, they almost exclusively tell the story of the minority members of that community—the white owners. (However, some plantations nowadays may have a small exhibit or two about the "enslaved" majority who lived there.)

Although blacks have always been a minority of the overall American population, the vast majority of people on America's plantations were always black. For example, The Hermitage plantation in Nashville says blacks typically made up 90% of their total population.

While Ernie and I were visiting The Hermitage, the plantation owned and operated by President Andrew Jackson, I picked up a pamphlet they offered, called *Beyond The Mansion*. It states:

> "By the 1840s, there were more than 150 African-American slaves living and working on the Hermitage plantation, by far the largest number of slaves on any farm in Davidson County."

This quote comes from The Hermitage's website:

> "In all reality, slavery was the source of Andrew Jackson's wealth. The Hermitage was a 1,000-acre, self-sustaining plantation that relied completely on the labor of enslaved African-American men, women, and children. They performed the hard labor that produced The Hermitage's cash crop, cotton. The more land Andrew Jackson accrued, the more slaves he procured to work it. Thus, the Jackson family's survival was made possible by the profit garnered from the crops worked by the enslaved on a daily basis."

> "When Andrew Jackson bought The Hermitage in 1804, he owned nine enslaved African-Americans. Just 25 years later that number had swelled to over 100 through purchase and reproduction. At the time of his death in 1845, Jackson owned approximately 150 people who lived and worked on the property."

The Hermitage pamphlet, *Beyond The Mansion*, also says:

> "Since there are few written accounts of slave life during this time, we rely on archaeological research conducted at the sites of slave dwellings to provide us with details of a life centered around hard work but steeped in a rich culture all its own."

Before leaving The Hermitage Plantation, Ernie and I went into the gift shop. She picked up a book called, *My Folks Don't Want Me To Talk About Slavery*. When I saw the title, I picked up a copy and read these two quote on the top of the back cover:

> "One day Grandpappy sassed Miss Polly White, and she told him that if he didn't behave hisself that she would put him in her pocket. Grandpappy was a big man, and I asked him how Miss Polly could do that. He said she meant that she would sell him, then put the money in her pocket. He never did sass Miss Polly no more." – Sarah Debro

> "Slavery was a bad thing, and freedom, of the kind we got, with nothing to live on, was bad. Two snakes full of poison." –Patsy Mitchner

Below the quotes I read this:

> "These eloquent words come from former slaves themselves—an important but long-neglected source of information about the institution of

slavery in the United States. Who could better describe what slavery was like than the people who experienced it? And describe it they did, in thousands of remarkable interviews sponsored by the federal Writers' Project during the 1930s."

Runaway slaves also wrote books about their personal experience of majority life on plantations. Several years ago, I read a collection of four slave narratives, *The Classic Slave Narratives*, edited by Henry Louis Gates. It opened my eyes to learn things about enslavement I never could have imagined. The first-hand descriptions of people's suffering and abuse tore my heart up. I wept many times while reading it.

Gates says:

> "The African-American slave narratives, were largely forgotten, devalued as literature or dismissed as valid historical evidence, until the first generation of black studies professors insisted on teaching them in the 1960s and 1970s. Even then, there were skeptics who felt that the slave narratives had little to no literary value, that if they were useful at all, it was for historical research."

Gates says there are more than 6,000 slave narratives and 204 known, book-length slave narratives. (So I wonder why The Hermitage pamphlet says, "Since there are few written accounts of slave life during this time, we rely on archaeological research.")

Goodreads says this about *The Classic Slave*

Narratives:

"No group of slaves anywhere, in any era, has left such prolific testimony to the horror of bondage as African-American slaves. Here are four of the most notable narratives quoted in the book *My Folks Don't Want Me To Talk About Slavery*: *The Life of Olaudah Equiano; The History of Mary Prince; Narrative of the Life of Frederick Douglass;* and *Incidents in the Life of Slave Girl*."

Another slave narrative, *12 Years A Slave,* by Solomon Northup, was recently made into a movie directed by Steve McQueen. It was a best seller when it was first-published in 1853 and became a present-day best seller when the movie was released. Northup was a free black man who was kidnapped by human traffickers in New York in 1841 and then sold "down the river" into slavery in Louisiana. There he was physically forced to do hard labor on plantations for 12 years until he managed to secretly send information to his family and friends in New York. With the help of the government, they were able to get him released. Here are a few quotes from a few, lesser known, slave narratives (slightly edited for grammar and wording):

"There was a jail on the place (the plantation near Camden, North Carolina that enslaved Trentham and about 400 others) to put slaves in and in the jail, there was a place to put your hands in, called stocks. Slaves were put there for punishment. I saw lots of slaves whipped by the overseers. The patrollers came round ever now and then and if you were off the plantation and had no pass, they tore you up with the lash."— Henry James Trentham

"About the worst thing I ever saw was a slave woman who had been sold off from her three-weeks-old baby; and was being marched (from North Carolina) to New Orleans. She had walked till she was give out; and she was weak enough to fall in the middle of the road. She was chained with twenty or thirty other slaves, and the speculators ate their dinner. The slaves weren't given anything to eat. As I passed by; this woman begs me in God's name for a drink of water and I give it to her. I ain't never been so sorry for nobody. It was in the month of August, and the sun was bearing down hot when the slaves and their drivers left the shade. They walked for a little piece, and the woman fell out. She died there on the side of the road, and right there they buried her, cussing, they told me about losing money on her."—Josephine Smith

"Master had his sweethearts among his slave women. I ain't no man for telling false stories, I tell the truth, and that is the truth. At that time, it was a hard job to find a master that didn't have (special) women among his slaves. That was a general thing among the slave owners. One of the slave girls on a plantation near us went to her missus (the slaveholder's white wife) and told her about her master forcing her to let him have something to do with her, and her missus told her, 'Well, go on, you belong to him.'" –Jacob

Manson

"Getting married and having a family was a joke in the days of slavery, as the main thing in allowing any form of matrimony among the slaves was to raise more slaves in the same sense and for the same purpose as stock raisers raise horses and mules, that is, for work. A woman who could produce fast was in great demand and would bring a good price on the auction block."—Thomas Hall

"Conditions and rules were bad, and the punishments were severe and barbarous. Some masters acted like savages. In some instances, slaves were burned at the stake. Families were torn apart by selling. Mothers were sold from their children. Children were sold from their mothers, and fathers were not considered in any way as a family part."—Thomas Hall

"Plenty of colored women (on plantations) had children by white men. She knew better than to not do what he said . . . Then they take them very same children what have their own blood and make slaves out of them."—W.L. Bost

Definition of Plantation

During the night after touring those three Nashville plantations, I woke up with these definitions going through my mind and got up about 3:15 am to write them down:

Plantation: A slave-labor camp established for

the purpose of building and maintaining a mansion, a large to huge farm, and a lavish lifestyle for one man, known as the *Master*, and the free, white members of his family.

Master: The legal owner, operator, and overlord (according to American law) of a for-profit, Antebellum forced-labor camp.

Antebellum: Pre-Civil War.

The three most famous American plantations belonged to American Presidents. They are Mount Vernon, owned and operated by George Washington; Monticello, designed, owned, and operated by Thomas Jefferson; and The Hermitage, owned and operated by Andrew Jackson.

(Of the first 12 American Presidents only two had never owned slaves. Of the first 16 only four had never owned slaves.)

Another famous, American plantation owner/operator was Patrick Henry, the prominent American Founding Father who ironically said:

"Give me liberty or give me death."

Although he personally enslaved people and forcibly made them work for him without pay, denying them their basic human rights, Henry also said:

"Liberty, the greatest of all earthly blessings—give us that precious jewel, and you may take everything else."

Vacationing in Chattanooga, Tennessee

About two weeks after the Nashville plantation visits, Ernie and I took a vacation trip to the Chattanooga, Tennessee area. When we arrived on a Sunday we were eating lunch while reading a local paper. As I was looking through it I noticed there were some Juneteenth celebrations going on. (On June 19, 1865, some American slaves in Texas got the word they were free and held a jubilee. They called it Juneteenth! It has become a day for celebrating the end of legal human trafficking in America.)

We felt like we were supposed to attend two of those events. The first was scheduled later that afternoon. It was a panel discussion about the black church. The panel consisted of two black pastors and one white pastor. They talked about how the black church was the only institution available for blacks to participate in during slavery and during Jim Crow segregation in the South.

They said because of that, the church and Christianity has always been a very important part of black culture and helped blacks survive under slavery and overcome the negative ideas and behaviors against their color.

They gave some examples from their personal experience. One black pastor said he was 50 and still remembers when he was 4 years old. A white church picked him up, along with some other children, in a bus for vacation Bible school. He said the pastor gathered the black children together and told them the Bible taught the *Curse of Ham* where black people were cursed by God and made to be servants. (I refuted that false idea earlier in this book.)

The other black pastor on the panel (who was 62) told how he was the only black child in his third-grade class. He said the teacher read a book about *Black Sambo* and kept showing cartoonish pictures of *Sambo* to the class. He said he wanted to hide, but he had nowhere to go.

As they continued the discussion, they said the concept of the black church was imposed on African-Americans because they generally were not allowed in the white church. They said they would love to see Christians in America united as one church. The white pastor said he wanted to see that as well, but he was recently saddened by a vote in his denomination about a simple resolution declaring racism to be a sin. He said it failed to pass.

A couple of days later we attended another Juneteenth event in Chattanooga. This was a lecture about the Cherokee removal on the *Trail of Tears* (in 1831) and the four thousand black slaves they took with them to Oklahoma. (I had heard about some Native Americans having slaves, but I didn't realize the *five civilized tribes* in the South had been very involved in holding and using slaves.)

The lecturer was a young, white National Park Ranger. He told how the Cherokees suffered and many died on the *Trail of Tears*. Then he asked us why we thought the Cherokee slave owners wouldn't just free their slaves, rather than forcing other human beings to suffer the trip with them. Someone answered, "Money." He agreed but said there were also laws in the Southern states which made the manumission of slaves (the act of freeing slaves) illegal.

He told about how, after they arrived in Indian Territory (which later became Oklahoma), the Cherokees continue to hold the slaves and use them in hard, agricultural labor until they finally freed them during the Civil War and called them *Freedmen*. They also officially made them full citizens of the Cherokee nation with full rights (eventually known as the "Black Indians"). However, soon afterwards, the Cherokee nation began to limit and take away the rights of the Freedmen.

Our lecturer, who grew up in Alabama, compared this with the parallel events about how, after 3 Amendments to the U.S. Constitution freed the slaves and gave blacks citizenship and voting rights, then the Southern states began to deny and take away those rights. This resulted in the harsh, Jim Crow discrimination which lasted until the Civil Rights Movement.

Afterwards, he asked for questions. The all white audience (except for one black lady) asked questions about the injustices done to the Cherokees, rather than about the main point of the lecture—how the Cherokees used and abused their black slaves and denied rights to the Freedmen. America's color-hierarchy seemed obvious during the questions, with Cherokees above blacks and *you-know-who* on the top. (As we have seen, 250 years of color-based slavery established a skin-hierarchy which, although legally ended, still lingers in our American psyche.)

Two days later we were in the small town of Lafayette, Georgia. We stopped at a city park to walk. As we walked around the park we came to a small log cabin, which I said looked like a slave cabin. Then we noticed a large house a little ways from the cabin. We approached the house from behind and found a historical marker called "African American Pioneers of the Marsh-Warthen-Clements house."

The marker said the house "was built by enslaved African Americans in an African cultural style known as the *Shot Gun*. Slaves traveled with Marsh from North Carolina and Covington, Georgia to Lafayette." It said:

> "In 1850 Marsh owned 12 slaves. In 1860 he owned 8 slaves that lived in two slave houses. One of Marsh's beloved slaves was Wiley Marsh, a mulatto, born circa 1834/1835."

Later I did some research and discovered the tiny log house was a replica of a slave house first owned by Spencer Marsh and built by his slaves. I also learned Wiley Marsh was probably Spencer Marsh's son who he held as a slave.

Skin Colors – Plantations - Chattanooga

7. The Meaning of Dr. King's Dream?

Creatively Thinking About Color-Kindness

Don't just focus on your own skin care. Care about the skin all other people live in by treating them with kindness and respect.

If the world only had one color, and just one shade of that color; how boring sight would be! Add a new color to humanity's array of skin colors—gold! Follow the Golden Rule with all colors of people: "Treat others the way you want to be treated."

One of the most important things to exclude from your thinking is skin-color-exclusion. To make someone an outsider is a real human divider. I've been included, and I've been excluded. I like inclusion better.

Why does the concept of race produce so much pain and confusion? Bottom line: Race is an illusion based on exclusion.

Racial categories are very inaccurate. Feelings and opinions about race are often way off base. Unfortunately, race is a fantasy that was enshrined as a reality, early in American history. Our society has been impacted by its consequences ever since.

People say, "Race is complicated," but it's really simple. It's the false belief skin color makes people different from you.

Sometimes what we call "color-blindness" is really a way to ignore and avoid the difficult issue of color animosity in America. Let's try not to do that. Sometimes prejudice is bold, aggressive, and sometimes it wears camouflage.

King's Dream of Not Being Judged by Color

Martin Luther King openly dreamed that such color-evaluation in America would stop. Was King referring to colorblindness when he said these famous words?

> "I have a dream that my four little children will one day live in a nation where they will not be judged by the color of their skin, but by the content of their character."

Colorblindness doesn't notice or acknowledge skin color or ethnic heritage. It looks right past them. Notice, King didn't say he dreamed the skin color of his children would not be noticed, but they wouldn't be judged by it.

I don't believe King wanted his children to lose or forget their skin color—their black heritage—and to be white-like. However, I do believe King's dream was that blackness would no longer be seen as a negative thing, as a degraded condition, in America. He wanted his children to be evaluated by the kind of people they are, not rejected, dismissed, or ignored because of what they look like.

Wouldn't our country be better off if blacks and whites were judged, categorized, and/or evaluated the same way? Today there is a double standard. Popular culture and public media tend to evaluate ordinary whites by their behavior, not by their skin color; however, ordinary blacks are often either ignored (a colorblind response) or described as *black* (a color-based response). However, the more society can see skin color, fully embrace and respect all shades as equally human, and relate to one another with heart-felt kindness, the better off we will all be.

Eye-Color-Blindness

You never hear about eye-color blindness. I've never heard anyone say, "I don't see eye-color!" Why? Because eye-color injustice is almost non-existent. I wish we could say the same for skin-color injustice. However, In America, there has been far more skin-color injustice than anybody realizes; far more than can ever be comprehended by a human mind.

Rather than trying to learn about and understand skin-color injustice, it's easier to be "colorblind" so you can't see it. However, denial doesn't change hidden facts. It just lets them simmer. Color-injustice has simmered for centuries and continues to simmer in the psyche of both black and white Americans (as ancestral embarrassment and shame in whites, and as ancestral hurt and anger in blacks). That's why racial anger and violence still erupt from time to time.

Skin-color is a natural part of people. However, the concept of race was man-made over centuries.

Therefore, it must be disassembled by people. That will take time. But it takes more than time. It requires openness, honesty, humility, discussion, new perspectives, healing, reconciliation, acknowledgment of past wrongdoing, new attitudes, historical corrections, and changes in society.

Time for Color-Appreciation

We do not need to be blind to color because color is not (and never has been) a problem. It's the negative interpretation of color that is the problem. Skin color is intrinsic, like eye color, but the concept of race is a manmade invention.

The physical differences between groups of people make them look a little different from other groups. Normal physical differences are real and should be appreciated, not denied. However, the idea normal physical differences effect the quality or value of a person is completely mythical. We do not need to try to avoid seeing color. Why?

Because colorblindness causes a variety of problems:

1) It ignores negative racial experiences.
2) It overlooks people's heritage.
3) It shoves aside people's cultural viewpoints.
4) It equates color with something negative (we need to be blind to that).
5) It is impossible for people who are not physically colorblind, not to see skin color, even if they say they don't.
6) It impedes the healthy discussion of race.

7) It devalues the stories and experience of people of color.
8) It too easily brushes aside the man-made issue of race, rather than dealing with the roots of the problem.

When we are colorblind, we are blind to the abuse of color, to the misuse of color, and to the ruse of color (a ruse is a deceptive stratagem or maneuver, a trick). We are also blind to the delight of color and to the insight of color. We do not need to be blind to color. We simply need to respond to color respectively and kindly. Whatever color a person wears on their skin, that person is still a valuable human being!

To get *beyond colorblindness to* **color-kindness**, we must not just ignore the stages of racial injustice but dismantle them. We need to be kind enough to face, examine, renounce, and dismantle the historical realities of color-devaluation, color-dehumanizing, color-disdain, color-abuse, color-cruelty, and color-injustice.

To be colorblind in a society built on a long history of color-injustice, is to silently side with that injustice. America has worked and passed many laws to try to overcome color-abuse . . . those laws have succeeded in numerous ways, so much so we seem to have moved beyond open racism into color-apathy. Perhaps now it's time to embrace color-appreciation.

We white people, who are unlikely to experience many serious disadvantages due to race, can effectively ignore racism in American life, justify the current social order, and feel more comfortable with our relatively privileged standing in society. So, it will take us some work, some effort, to appreciate the culture and experiences of African-Americans. But try we must.

Color-Kindness Challenge

Here is a formula for racial healing and reconciliation:

Color + racial feelings = stress and awkwardness

but

Color + kindness = peace and joy!

What does color-kindness look like? How can all humans be color-kind instead of color-blind? How can we show color-appreciation instead of color apathy? Here are some ideas.

Color-kindness looks like any other act of kindness except it is kindness shown to someone of a different color (or ethnicity) than yourself. Color-kindness is intentionally being kind to someone who socially or culturally wouldn't normally expect kindness, time, and attention from you.

In recent years many Americans have become intentionally military-kind. I see it and hear it a lot. I will be in a public place and a stranger will walk up to someone in a military uniform and sincerely say, "Thank you for your service." Sometimes that is all that happens, but even then, I can see the military person appreciates the act of kindness. At other times the two people will engage in a pleasant conversation.

If millions of Americans can learn to show military-kindness, then why isn't it possible that millions of us learn to show color-kindness? If we can do random acts of kindness, then why isn't it possible to do intentional acts of color-kindness?

So, what could you say and/or do to show kindness to someone of a different skin-tone than you? Here are a few suggestions.

- Greet and be warm and friendly to people of every shade and tint (especially those of a different hue than you). Start a friendly conversation with them.
- Offer color-kindness by giving a sincere compliment: "I love your hair," or "That's a beautiful shirt (or blouse)," or "Those are some nice shoes," or some other compliment.
- Show color-kindness by intentionally doing a good deed for someone of a different shade: Hold a door open. Pick up something they dropped. Let them go in front of you in traffic.
- Demonstrate color-kindness by writing someone a note, sending them a card, paying for their coffee or meal, or giving them a small gift.
- Offer color-kindness by giving differently tinted people some of your time and attention. Sincerely listen to their story and really hear where they are coming from. Show interest as

they share.
- Show color-kindness by learning about people of other colors. Read books about different colors of people. Research color groups on the internet.
- Invite someone of different color to your home for coffee, tea, or a meal.
- Visit an organization or church, mosque, or temple of a different color group.
- Every time you encounter someone of a different color than yourself, think, "How can I show **intentional color-kindness** right now?" You may be surprised at the creative ideas that come into your mind.
- Determine to be intentionally color-kind as often as possible.
- Try to make a differently shaded person you encounter feel better for seeing you.
- Avoid color-blindness. Instead, notice the differences and find a way to appreciate the variety of people who you see throughout the day.

A Few Kindness Quotes and Comments

"Kindness in words creates confidence. Kindness in thinking creates profoundness. Kindness in giving creates love."—Lao Tzu – Great words of color-kindness from an ancient Chinese man.

"Be kind whenever possible. It is always possible."—Tenzin Gyatso, 14th Dalai Lama – Can you feel this color-kindness coming from the world-wide leader of Buddhism?

> "Be a rainbow in someone else's cloud."—Maya Angelou – Beautiful advice from a wonderful black poet.
>
> "A single act of kindness throws out roots in all directions, and the roots spring up and make new trees." – Amelia Earhart – Encouraging words about the power of kindness from a world-renown woman pilot.
>
> "Do your little bit of good where you are; it's those little bits of good put together that overwhelm the world."—Desmond Tutu – Powerful kindness insights from an African.
>
> "Kindness and politeness are not overrated at all. They're underused." Tommy Lee Jones – And common-sense kindness from a white guy.

You have the power of color-kindness. Why not use it today?

Color-Blindness Quotes and Comments

> "Colorblindness derails the process of addressing racism before it has even started."—Jon Greenberg – We can't talk effectively about situations and experiences that we won't see. It's difficult to show color-kindness (and compassion) to people if you're unaware of their color-based hurts and struggles.
>
> "To overcome racism, one must first take race into account."—Harry Blackmun, Supreme Court

Justice – Most people will admit that America has racial problems today, yet a lot of people do not want to talk openly about many of the historical, racial facts which produced those problems. Can racial problems exist without the existence of racism? Can they be solved without acknowledging it?

"People notice if you are black. People notice if you are female. We are certainly not either colorblind or gender-blind in this country."—Condoleezza Rice – Noticing skin color is not a problem. However, evaluating people by it and categorizing them by it is.

"I am asking you not to be colorblind, but to be color-brave."—Melanie Hobson – America needs color-brave pioneers to intentionally forge new trails beyond the familiar, ineffective color pathways we blindly continue to follow.

"Colorblind racism is the new racial music most people dance to, the 'new racism' is subtle, institutionalized and seemingly nonracial."—Eduardo Bonilla Silva – Does racism have to be intentional? Or can un-sightedness, unawareness, and passivity be a type of racism?

"Never trust someone who says they don't see color. This means to them, you are invisible."—Nayyirah Waheed – If we do not see the differences between us and others, we aren't very curious about them. We assume they are just like us and so we don't ask them about their lives and we don't really get to know them or their perspectives.

"Colorblind ideology was a very effective adaptation to the challenges of the Civil Rights Era. Colorblind ideology allows society to deny the reality of racism in the face of its persistence, while making it more difficult to challenge than when it was openly espoused."—Robin DiAngelo – If we don't see color, then we don't feel a need to deal with issues of color.

"The conundrum of the twenty-first (century) is that with the best intentions of color blindness, and laws passed in this spirit, we still carry instincts and reactions inherited from our environments and embedded in our being below the level of conscious decision. There is a color line in our heads."—Krista Tippett – Color-blindness lets our unconscious struggles with color stay nicely tucked away; unresolved.

"Let's break it down into simple terms: Color-Blind equals, 'People of color, we don't see you (at least not that bad colored part).' As a person of color, I like who I am, and I don't want any aspect of that to be unseen or invisible. The need for colorblindness implies there is something shameful about the way God made me and the culture I was born into, that we shouldn't talk about. Thus, colorblindness has helped make race into a taboo topic that polite people cannot openly discuss. And if you can't talk about it, you can't understand it, much less fix the racial problems that plague our society."—Monnica T.

Williams – Colorblindness makes it a taboo to talk about the issues people of color struggle with every day; and makes their inner healing very difficult by basically telling them to just "get over it."

Fun Skin Facts Cultivating Skin-Color-Appreciation

- ❖ The color of people's skin has nothing to do with their intelligence, personality, attitude, cleanliness, or health.

- ❖ Skin accounts for only about 15% of the body's weight and 0% of a human soul. Perhaps evaluating people by skin color isn't wise. "I am not this skin. I am the soul that lives within."—India Arie

- ❖ Skin is actually an organ—the largest organ in the body. The color of people's skin is their organ donation from God. Try not to belittle their gift!

- ❖ Skin is our bodyguard. It protects our internal organs, bones, and muscles from disease and infection. Like any bodyguard, skin should be evaluated by its effectiveness, not by its color.

- ❖ The average person has more than 18 square feet of skin. That's enough skin to make a 6 by 3 billboard for justice saying: "Respect me, because I've got skin in the game of life just like you do!"

- There are countless nerve endings in skin that continually respond to temperature and pressure. People's skin is sensitive, show respect.

- Skin is the body's thermostat. It releases sweat to cool the body down and regulates temperature by detecting hot and cold. Although skin is insulation, it can't insulate the soul from negative comments about race.

- All skin produces melanin, a chemical that determines the skin's color. Different amounts of melanin in different people create the different skin colors of humanity. It is also what creates freckles. Melanin is built-in sunscreen. The more you have of it, the more effectively your skin copes with sunlight. "One day our decedents will think it incredible that we paid so much attention to things like the amount of melanin in our skin."—Franklin A. Thomas

- A person's skin continually sheds dead skin cells (about 9 pounds of dead skin a year) and is constantly creating new skin cells. The entire skin is renewed about every 28 days. Let's be like skin and shed the dead racial beliefs that haven't worked well and create some new beliefs that release skin-appreciation for all colors.

- Eleven miles of blood vessels run through the skin. No matter what the skin's color, prick it and it bleeds red!

- When exposed to repeated friction, skin becomes callus. When exposed to racial friction, try not to let your heart become callus.

- Skin attempts to heal itself by forming scar tissue. See your racial scars as a sign of healing.

- Every inch of skin has its own stretchiness and strength designed especially for its specific location on the body. So, the skin you have on your stomach is very different in elasticity and strength when compared with the skin that you have on your elbows. Since our skin is designed to be flexible according to different needs, shouldn't we be flexible when we encounter people of different skin colors?

- The surface of the skin is the home to millions of colonies of bacteria. Be like bacteria. They don't discriminate against the color of people's skin.

- The scientific name of skin is *Cutaneous Membrane*. To appreciate people regardless of the color of their Cutaneous Membrane seems like a no-brainer.

- Artificial skin has been produced by using

silicon and bovine collagen. This artificial skin can be used for complete skin replacement. Rather than replacing your skin, learn to appreciate the skin you're in.

- ❖ The average person has about 300 million skin cells. A single square inch of skin has about 19 million cells and up to 300 sweat glands. Don't look down on anyone's skin cells!

- ❖ Skin is thickest on the bottom of the feet. So, to heal and protect your racial hurts cover them with the thick skin from your heel!

- ❖ Skin can pour out as much as 3 gallons of sweat per day. The sweat, the time, the devotion to liberty and justice for all regardless of skin shade, pays off!

The Meaning of Dr. King's Dream?

8. Heroes of Liberty & Justice for All

More Original Thoughts

To be a true believer in "liberty and justice for all," I have to care about how everyone is treated, not just those who look like me. If "all men are created equal," I should not treat people any differently based on skin shade.

The concept of *rights* is not a new idea. The American Declaration of Independence states that people have "inalienable rights." Speaking up for rights is as American as it gets! Any rights I deserve, others deserve.

Reading black history helped me develop color-appreciation, color-compassion, and color-kindness. I've discovered that much wisdom is unheard if I stay stuck in my herd. Here are some more "liberty and justice for all" heroes!

Remembering an American Atrocity

I once stood in a small cemetery where a little-known group of American hostages are buried. There are no tombstones, only a flat rock placed on each grave—no names to identify these Americans who suffered tremendous indignities and deprivations as forced laborers. It was a horrible atrocity in American history.

Cars whiz by the small wooded area where these 20 or so Americans are buried, but no one seems to notice. There are no flags, no flowers. The graves had been forgotten for a while and were only discovered when road builders were working to widen the road. So, they paved around the trees and the graves and now these abused Americans are buried in the median of a road that runs in front of a school.

My heart grieved as I stood there and thought about how these Americans suffered. I wanted to do something, but I didn't know what to do. So, I knelt and prayed and quietly left.

I think of that cemetery often and of the horrors suffered by those forgotten Americans. What is the proper response to injustices after the victims have died? I think few of the people who drive by have any idea about what cruelty was done by their countrymen to those buried Americans.

Maybe someday you can visit this unnamed cemetery. It's not hard to find. It is not in Afghanistan or Iraq or Lebanon or Syria or Iran or Vietnam or Cambodia. It is not in Korea or Germany or Japan. It is in Brentwood, Tennessee, just down from Brentwood High School in the wooded median of the road.

These 20 or so Americans suffered at the hands of their fellow Americans. They were forced to do a lifetime of hard labor against their will. They were bought and sold and treated like horses or oxen. They had no rights—no freedom—not even a proper burial. For the most part their only escape from their suffering was death. Their plight was sanctioned by the US government and even by many religious denominations.

As I stand in the cemetery and look at the graves, I can imagine the American men, women, and children . . . their hopelessness, their pain, their despair, their constant humiliation, their tears, their prayers. And I understand . . . Slavery was a genuine atrocity done to real people right here in our homeland.

Why don't you visit this cemetery? Come, see the graves of these forgotten Americans. Feel their history. Let it sink in. Come, bring flowers to honor in death those who received no honor in life. Bring tears to identify with fellow human beings who were crushed by American democracy. Bring prayers to ask for forgiveness and healing from the great evil done on American soil. Bring a friend (if you are white bring a black friend and if you are black, bring a white one).

The Vietnam Veterans Memorial helps people heal. They face reality—their pain, their sins. They repent, they forgive. They move forward. This unnamed slave cemetery can do the same.

Tennessee's Abolitionist Newspaper

Here's a little-known fact of American history and black history. Some white Southerners were boldly against slavery. In the early 1800s there was an anti-slavery movement in the South. Color-kind, Elihu Embree, started an anti-slavery newspaper, *The Emancipator,* around 1820 in East Tennessee. Because of stiff opposition the movement died out and most of its leaders were forced to move to free states.

Here are some quotations taken from Tennessee's abolitionist newspaper:

> "Here we behold human beings sold like herds of cattle — children torn by violence from their parent and sold in distant lands; matrimonial ties disregarded."–Manumission Society of Tennessee
>
> "Endeavor to know what is right, and to do it, dreading no consequences. Do good because it is good, not because men call it so."–Elihu Embree
>
> "I have never been able to discover that the author of nature intended that one complexion of the human skin should stand higher in the scale of being than another."–Elihu Embree
>
> "The practice of reducing our fellow men to a state of abject slavery is repugnant to the principles of the Christian religion."–Manumission Society of Tennessee
>
> "Christians appear to be fond of enslaving their fellow men and of growing rich off the spoil."–Stephen Brooks
>
> "Slaves are being degraded in their own estimation by being held slaves."–Elihu Embree
>
> "Through slavery men certainly sin against light and knowledge and are using the most probable means of drawing down the judgments of

Heaven upon our guilty land."–Stephen Brooks

"To my shame be it said that I have owned slaves. I always believed slavery to be wrong but had a tendency to not be very scrupulous in adhering to what I believed to be right. I repent that I ever owned one."–Elihu Embree

"I must insist upon it, that every friend of slavery is the enemy to American liberty, for American liberty is founded on the rights of man as expressed in the Declaration of Independence – 'that all men are by nature equally free.'"–The Emancipator

"It is said by some that they use their slaves well, but how a man could use me well by depriving me of my liberty and entailing the same infamy on my posterity to the latest generation, I am at a loss to conjecture."–Manumission Society of Tennessee

"I believe it has never yet been the lot of any writer or speaker to please everybody; why then should I be vain enough to expect such an attainment?" –Elihu Embree

America's Forgotten Freedom Fighters

How many times have you heard the Lee Greenwood song declaring: "I'm proud to be an American where at least I know I'm free. And I won't forget the men who died to give that right to me." However, we Americans have forgotten many men and women who fought and died to make us free. If we are going to honor those who chose to use violence to fight for freedom, shouldn't we be consistent and honor all of those who fought for freedom in America?

Take **Elijah Lovejoy** for instance. He was a Presbyterian minister who published a religious newspaper called *The St. Louis Observer*. After seeing Francis J. McIntosh, a slave, burned at the stake, Lovejoy began to write editorials against slavery. His press was wrecked by a mob in July 1836, so he moved to Alton, Illinois. There he continued writing and publishing against slavery even though his press was destroyed three more times. On November 7, 1837 Elijah Lovejoy and twenty of his friends were guarding a new press. That night they were attacked by a pro-slavery mob and Elijah Lovejoy died for liberty and justice all– killed by a shotgun blast.

How about **Nat Turner**? He was being held in lifelong bondage in Southampton County, Virginia. After much prayer, Turner made the courageous decision to do what the colonies did and fight for his freedom. On the morning of August 21, 1831, Turner and six followers began to attack slaveholders and to liberate their fellow slaves. After 40 hours Turner and his growing band of freedom fighters were attacked by an army of 3000 soldiers and more than 200 brave black Americans were killed. Turner escaped but was later captured and hanged–dying to give that right (freedom) to us all. His death was a turning point in our history and helped fuel the antislavery movement.

What about the hundreds, if not thousands of Americans who were killed running away from lifelong bondage? Courageous Underground Railroad conductors like **Harriet Tubman** highlight runaway slave successes, but what about all those who were killed while fleeing, or tortured to death when recaptured? Has our nation not forgotten the runaways who died for freedom? Is there even one monument to them anywhere in our country?

I'm so glad that there is a plan to put Harriet Tubman on the USA $20 bill! These forgotten American freedom fighters deserve great recognition.

Frederick Douglas

One such heroic runaway was Frederick Douglas. He was claimed to be a white guy's personal property from his birth around 1818 in the state of Maryland. He was physically, mentally, and emotionally abused—kept in degraded conditions and treated like an animal. Douglas was separated from his family and forcibly made to do manual labor without pay. He was not allowed to learn to read, but he found a way to do so without getting caught.

When he was 20 Douglas courageously escaped from his bondage. He began to tell people about what he went through. Without hatred, Douglas spoke with passion and authority about the horrors inflicted on him. The stories of his unjust suffering moved people deeply. Eventually he was asked to speak at meetings where he became known as a great American orator.

Throughout the rest of his life, Douglas continued to speak out against the horrible injustices of human slavery. He was a great American leader and was very active in the American antislavery movement.

For Frederick Douglas, the words "all men are created equal" were not just words in the Declaration of Independence to be overlooked in order to justify the cruelties of American slavery, but a passionate belief on which he heroically stood all of his life. Here are a few quotations from Frederick Douglas.

> "The limits of tyrants are prescribed by the endurance of those whom they oppose."
>
> "Wherever men oppress their fellows, wherever they enslave them, they will endeavor to find the needed apology for such enslavement and oppression in the character of the people oppressed and enslaved."
>
> "The thing worse than rebellion is the thing that causes rebellion."
>
> "Those who profess to favor freedom, and yet depreciate agitation, are men who want crops without plowing up the ground."
>
> "I prefer to be true to myself, even at the hazard of incurring the ridicule of others, rather than to be false, and to incur my own abhorrence."

"The soul that is within me no man can degrade."

Sojourner Truth

Another great American defender of liberty and justice for all was a woman named **_Sojourner Truth_**. She is a rock star of both black history and American history. She got away from slavery in the early 1800s and began to preach across the land. She was a powerful and passionate speaker and was frequently invited to speak for antislavery meetings and in meetings for women's rights.

So, where did Sojourner get her now famous name? She said that God gave it to her:

> "The Lord gave me the name *Sojourner* because I was to travel up and down the land showing the people their sins and being a sign unto them. Afterward I told the Lord I wanted another name because everybody had two names; and the Lord gave me *Truth*, because I was to declare the truth to the people."

This woman heard from God and then obeyed. She had no education, no financial backing. She was a former slave and belonged to America's most persecuted color group. She was bold and spoke the truth, openly telling people their sins of human trafficking and calling on them to stop doing wrong and turn to God. Yet, Sojourner Truth became world famous in her time and is still referred to in most American history books.

How we need people in our time who will listen to

God and boldly do what He tells them to. And that's the truth!

Uncle Tom's Cabin by Harriet Beecher Stowe

Harriet Beecher Stowe was a white woman who dared to write a novel in 1852, depicting the real horrors of slaveholding. It was about the many cruelties and injustices done to a man and his family, who she called *Uncle Tom*.

When, as an adult, I finally read *Uncle Tom's Cabin*, I was shocked to learn that Uncle Tom was no *Uncle Tom*. He was not weak or servile. He was not a wimp. He didn't cooperate with his owners for selfish reasons or for personal advantage.

Uncle Tom was strong, and he stood his ground. He frequently sacrificed his personal needs for the benefit of other slaves. He absolutely refused to disobey his conscience no matter what it cost him. He was so deeply principled that he refused to tell what he knew about two runaways even when he knew it meant he would be beaten to death.

Most of all, Uncle Tom was a sincere Christ-follower. He prayed, preached, and lived the Gospel. He was a true saint. Uncle Tom reminded me of Martin Luther King, Jr. He refused to cooperate with evil and he refused to do violence to others. He gave his life rather than compromise his faith or his principles. He was a martyr for Christ.

The two men who murdered Tom were the real *Uncle Toms*. The slaves Quimbo and Sambo were slave owner, Simon Legree's, overseers. They ruled, tortured, drove, and abused the other slaves for Simon Legree's favors like power, alcohol, and sex.

Harriet Beecher Stowe deeply grieved over the horrors of slavery. She said:

> "There is more done with pens than with swords."

She wrote to change the attitudes of people about slavery and she succeeded. Uncle Tom's Cabin sold two million copies in two years and greatly increased the antislavery feelings in America. Abraham Lincoln called her "the little woman who wrote the book that made this great war."

The *Weekly Call*, a black owned newspaper, wrote in 1896:

> "This book did more than any other agency to arouse the spirit of the people of the north against the system of slavery. If the merits of the book are to be determined by the nobleness of its aim and the purity of its purpose, and the extent to which they are accomplished, *Uncle Tom's Cabin* is the greatest production in American literature."

As I read about Uncle Tom and the other characters I was moved to tears at their pain and suffering and at the coldness and cruelty of their owners. Uncle Tom had three owners. Two were *kind (at least as kind as a human trafficker can be)* and one, Simon Lagree, was evil. His first owner got in financial trouble and sold Tom away from his wife and children (not much color-kindness in that). His second owner died suddenly—Tom and all the other slaves were sold.

Tom's third owner tormented and tortured Tom—eventually, had Tom killed. Stowe shows the system of slavery was so evil even *kind* owners caused tremendous pain and suffering. It is hard to believe such a cruelty was embraced and practiced by Americans for two hundred and fifty years.

In her last chapter, Harriet Beecher Stowe asks:

> "Does not every American Christian owe to the African race some effort at reparation for the wrongs that the American nation has brought upon them?"

Unfortunately, that reparation never came, and blatant racism and cruelty continued until the 1960s.

Today, race is still an issue. What are we to do? Harriet Beecher Stowe said this:

> "There is one thing that every individual can do– they can feel right. An atmosphere of sympathetic influence encircles every human being; and the man or woman who feels strongly, healthily and justly, on the great interests of humanity, is a constant benefactor to the human race. Are your feelings in harmony with the feelings of Christ? Or are they swayed and perverted by the sophistries of worldly policy?"

Christ wants us all to be one—to love one another. Yet how can we love people we do not know as friends, people we choose not to associate with? How can I love someone and not care about things that concern him?

We can't fix the past. But we can care about what it has led us to today. We can repent. We can forgive. We can understand. We can feel, and we can heal. We can build a future. We can discover God's treasure in our brothers and sisters of a different race.

Black Like Me by John Howard Griffin

Black Like Me is the story of how **John Howard Griffin**, a white man, took a drug that colored his skin black and traveled around the segregated, Jim Crow South in the late 1950s. The cover reads: "What was it like, really like to be black in the Deep South? Novelist John Howard Griffin darkened his skin and set out to discover by personal experience the night side of American life. This is his startling report." *Black Like Me* sold more than 10 million copies.

John Howard Griffin changed nothing but the color of his skin. However, that was enough to almost get him killed. He was continually mistreated, called names, given hateful looks, and despised for nothing other than his darkened skin color.

This is a side of American history that has been played down, forgotten, or hidden in our day. *Black*

Like Me brings to light the truth of American segregation, persecution, racism, and Jim Crow laws.

The experience changed Griffin and charged him up for justice and human rights. Afterward he became a prominent leader in the Civil Rights Movement. John Howard Griffin was a courageous and great American hero who is mostly forgotten in our day.

Read his book and you will be amazed how badly our country treated millions of its citizens for nothing more than skin color. You will also be inspired by the love, courage, and commitment of a man who believed the Declaration of Independence that "all men are created equal" enough to risk his life to personally learn about the racial injustice of our country. And after he learned about it, Griffin personally put his life on the line many times protesting for human rights in America.

Pudd'nhead Wilson, by Mark Twain

Pudd'nhead Wilson is the story of two boys. One was born into slavery, although he only had 1/32 black ancestry and was 31/32 white. (The slave laws mandated that the child of a slave woman was also a slave, even if he/she looked white.) The other boy was the white son of the master of the house.

The slave mother, Roxy, was caring for both boys. Here is what Mark Twain wrote about her: "To all intents and purposes Roxy was as white as anybody, but the one sixteenth of her which was black outvoted the other fifteen parts and made her a

Negro. She was a slave, and salable as such."

When Roxy heard that some fellow slaves were almost sold "down the river" to a slaveholder in the Deep South, she took drastic action to protect her son. The two babies looked similar, so she decided to switch them without the master's knowledge. As they grew up in each other's social and family position, they took on each other's roles.

The story takes place in the fictional town of Dawson's Landing, Missouri during the early Nineteenth Century. Before the switch, a young white lawyer, David Wilson, moves to town. Early on he makes a joke that the townspeople don't understand, so they believe he is mentally slow and give him the name *Pudd'nhead Wilson*. Wilson has a hobby of collecting fingerprints, which the local people also find very strange. At one point when Roxy is walking the babies before the switch, he asks her if he can fingerprint both babies—so, she gives him their correct names.

The story jumps forward about 20 years and Roxy's son, now known as Tom Driscoll (the deceased master's son) sincerely believes he is white. He is now the master of all the slaves. This causes him to act like a spoiled aristocrat. The real master's son is now known as Chambers (Roxy the slave's son) and is a slave on the plantation."

Eventually Pudd'nhead Wilson's fingerprints come to light and reveal the switch. After a complicated plot, Tom is returned to slavery and Chambers (the real Tom) is restored to his rightful position as the plantation owner. However, he struggles greatly, feeling intense unease in white society. He also loses all his black, slave friends, because as a white man, he is forbidden from socializing with them.

In this book, Mark Twain courageously shows how any perceived inferiority of American slaves was due to the way they were abused, humiliated, kept from any education, and treated as animals. A white man treated the same way wouldn't be any different.

James McCune Smith

Dr. James McCune Smith was a great American who overcame tremendous obstacles to become a first in American history—the first black medical doctor. He was born a slave in 1813. He received his freedom as a result of the Emancipation Act of the State of New York which freed all of the slaves in New York on July 4, 1827.

Smith said as a slave he "lived in the gloom of midnight, seemingly hopeless, dark and seemingly rayless." He said New York Emancipation Day "was a proud day, never to be forgotten by young lads."

After freedom, Smith became an apprentice to a blacksmith. He had a great hunger for education, so he studied as he worked. In the evenings and on Sundays he learned Greek and Latin because he wanted to go to medical school and those languages were required.

He applied to two American medical schools but was turned down because of his skin color.

However, the University of Glasgow in Scotland admitted him. He received his MD in 1837 making him the first African American physician. He returned to New York City and opened a successful medical and surgical practice at 93 West Broadway.

James McCune Smith was also an anti-human-trafficking activist and an essayist. He wrote for several black and anti-slavery newspapers. Here are some quotations from Dr. Smith:

> "People frown upon the works of their Creator—upon their fellow creatures, not for the hue of the soul, but of the skin."
>
> "Public opinion is the king of today and rules the land."
>
> "Like causes under like circumstances will produce like effects."
>
> "The Constitution of these United States holds that there are some 'other persons'—besides all men—who are not entitled to rights. We are these 'other persons'—we are the exception. It is our destiny to prove this exception is wrong and therefore contrary to the highest interests of the whole people."
>
> "Learned men in their rage for classification and from a reprehensible spirit to bend science to provoke peculiar prejudices, have brought the human spirit under the yoke of classification and have placed us in the very lowest rank."

Am I Related to American Hero, William Simms?

Twenty-year-old William Simms was being held captive against his will. Although he had never committed a crime or been in a military setting, he was being human trafficked and forced to do hard labor with six other captives.

The people holding them prisoner and making them work were led by a woman named Mrs. Mason. One of the captives overheard one of their captors say:

> "When this job is done, I'll destroy that breed o' dogs."

So, William Simms and the six others decided that their best chance for survival was to attempt an escape. They knew if they were recaptured they would either be killed or tortured.

The seven fled on foot, leaving on a Saturday night and following a mountain range that they knew led to the border and to their freedom. They traveled only at night, lying up in the woods during the day. The weather was cold, wet, and there was some snow.

Their meager provisions quickly gave out; after several days they were nearly starving. William Simms later said he was so exhausted he had to crawl on his hands and knees to relieve his feet. Four of them were caught, but Simms and two others made it to freedom in 1858 with help from the Underground Railroad.

William Simms later married and settled in South Danby, New York, where he rented land and farmed. He is remembered because a fifteen-year-old white boy, Arthur Charles Howland, who lived on a neighboring farm, interviewed him and took notes about Simms' escape from slavery.

I was moved by William Simms' story. We share the same last name and it is possible I am related to him. I am descended from four Northern Irish Simms brothers who initially settled in North Carolina in the 1780s. "William" is a common name in our family tree (I am related to the famous American author and human trafficker, William Gilmore Simms). William Simms escaped from slavery on a farm in Virginia.

Simms' story is just one of the many thousands of American heroes who risked their lives in attempts to escape from being held and trafficked as human property. Many were killed. Many were tortured. Many were "sold down the river" to even more cruelty and torture in the Deep South. And many, like Simms, made their escape. But they all took heroic action in the name of freedom.

Has anyone better lived out Patrick Henry's cry (who himself held innocent people in life-long forced labor): "Give me liberty or give me death," than America's runaway slaves? Frederick Douglas, perhaps the most famous runaway slave; said:

> "In coming to the fixed determination to run away from slavery, we did more than Patrick

Henry. With us it was a doubtful liberty at most, and almost certain death if we failed."

Harriet Tubman said:

"There was one of two things I had a right to, liberty or death. If I could not have one, I would have the other."

Throughout our history, many Americans have risked much for freedom–the Founding Fathers, Patriots, Abolitionists, Underground Railroad Conductors, the men and women of our Armed Forces–all stood up courageously for the cause of individual liberty. There are many monuments and memorials to them in our country. But where are the monuments to the great courage and heroism of America's runaway slaves?

Thank you, William Simms, for your brave stand for freedom! Sincerely, Steve Simms.

9. Leaving the Lie: Blackness, Being Unracist

Race Comments Never Said Like This Before

Here's a simple life improvement hint: Never vent about people because of the tint of the skin tent they live in. Skin color makes a much better tapestry than it does a battle plan.

Let's color outside the maligns of racial put-downs and stereotypes and move beyond taking cues from skin hues. The engine which drives the myth of race is the negative definition attached to certain skin colors.

Every race needs a finish line; so, let's finish with the myth of color-based race and embrace each other's as members of the human family! No one should have to go to a dermatologist to be told their skin color is not a malady!

The tint of a person's skin reveals nothing about the intent of his heart. Red and yellow, black and white; we all have a deep need to be appreciated.

Refuting America's Big Lie About Blackness

Black is beautiful! To retailers in America, Black Friday is the most wonderful day of the year—the day after Thanksgiving Day when their businesses begin to turn a profit for the year.

It's an honor to have a black belt or to be invited to a black-tie affair. Much of what the American Baby

Boomers know, they learned off a blackboard, not a computer. Financially, we're all like retailers—we want to be in the black! (Henry Ford said: "Give me any color, as long as it is black.")

Black opal has the most brilliant colors and is the costliest type of opal there is. Black tea is the world's most popular tea. When ordering coffee, it has always been popular to boldly proclaim: "I'll take mine black!"

Yosef A. A. Ben-Jochannan described black skin as: "Dipped in chocolate, bronzed in elegance, enameled with grace, toasted with beauty."

The prophet Jeremiah asked: "Can the Ethiopian change his skin or the leopard his spots?" Of course not. It is a gift from God.

Why would an Ethiopian even want to change his skin? Perhaps because of the way he was treated, labeled, abused, misunderstood, or rejected because of his skin color?

Black skin is black beauty because God made it! To judge skin and overlook the person within is an outrageous sin against God.

For thousands of years oil was seen to be something ugly that ruined the land and made it worthless. Today we see oil as *black* gold, for the amazing treasure that it is.

Beautiful black light shines throughout American history and into our present day. Can you see it?

Brilliant black light shining brightly–your vast accomplishments have remained largely unnoticed, unappreciated, and unvalued.

Lord, forgive us for believing the lie that taught us black people are inferior. Help us repent. Set our country free from that lie. Open our hearts to deeply believe "all means all" and to live out our national creed that says: "ALL men are created equal."

You Might be Unracist IF...

The clear majority of Americans claim (and believe) they are unracist; they believe they are "colorblind." However, in an unracist society, race is appreciated, not just ignored.

You might be unracist if you have gone beyond being colorblind, to being color-kind.

You might be unracist if laundry is the only thing you separate by color.

You might be unracist if you are like a panda. They're not stuck in one category. They're black and white and Asian.

You might be unracist if the only race you don't have love and compassion for, is the one you have to run.

You might be unracist if you think racial profiling is collecting dossiers about NASCAR drivers.

You might be unracist if you embrace all peoples as

your equals regardless of their race.

You might be unracist if a person's heart means more to you than his/her appearance.

You might be unracist if you're convinced that pigment does not and never has made a person.

You might be unracist if you reach out and actively show love to people the world says you should hate.

You might be unracist if you recognize America's racist past established belief systems and institutions that still, silently promote racism today (even in your own heart).

You might be unracist if you believe racism is never justifiable; past, present, or future.

You might be unracist if you realize that to ignore someone because of race is just as racist as to be intentionally mean to someone because of race.

You might be an unracist if you are on a lifetime journey of love and equality for all shades of humanity.

You might be unracist if you don't make generalizations about groups of people.

You might be unracist if you continually search for the smallest remnants of racial prejudice in your own heart and instantly uproot them the moment you see them.

You might be unracist if you speak up against injustice and racism wherever it occurs.

You might be unracist if you can talk about people who look different than you do and not mention race or ethnicity.

You might be unracist if you don't think your color neighborhood is the safest.

You might be unracist if people's skin color matters no more to you than their eye color.

You might be unracist if you never use (or think) racial slurs.

You might be unracist if your church congregation has no segregation.

You might be unracist if black history, white history, native history, and every other color of your nation's history are all important to you.

Racial Reconciliation in the 1800s

"Multiracial church" is a Twenty-First Century concept. However, did you know there was a multiracial church with about 2,000 members (reported to have 1/3 white members), led by a black man and former slave in Richmond, Virginia in the 1880s? It was called Sixth Street Mount Zion Baptist Church and it still exists today.

Mount Zion was founded on September 3, 1867. Its first meeting place was an abandoned Confederate horse stable on Brown's Island in the James River.

After a few short years and several moves, Sixth Mount Zion owned a beautiful brick building, located in what was known at the time as *Little Africa*. The building had more than 1,000 seats on the first floor and had modern gas lights. For more than 30 years, until his death in 1901 at the age of 88, **Rev. John Jasper** preached and ministered to both black and white people from the pulpit of Mount Zion and both far and wide.

Rev. John Jasper was born a slave on the 4th of July 1812 on Peachy Plantation near Richmond. He was the youngest of 24 children. John Jasper's father, who had died two months before his birth, had predicted his last child would be a great preacher.

As a young man, John was sold and worked in his new master's tobacco factory. When he was 27, after "seeking God six long weeks," John had a life changing encounter with Jesus Christ and began to shout around the tobacco factory. As he shared his conversion experience with his coworkers, his master, Samuel Hardgrove, heard the commotion and came out of his office to see what was happening.

John told him he had become a Christian. Later John recounted: "Then master Sam did a thing that nearly made me drop to the floor. He walked over to me and gave me his hand and said: "John, I wish you mighty well. Your Savior is mine, and we are brothers in the Lord."

John Jasper continues: "Master Sam's face was raining tears and he said; 'John you needn't work anymore today. I'm giving you a holiday. Go tell your mother, go to your neighbors and tell them; go anywhere you want to and tell them the good news. It'll do you good and do them good. Keep telling it, John, wherever you go, tell it!'"

After that, John began to preach in a slave church on the Peachy Plantation. As the slave church grew, whites from the area began to attend. When Dr. Benjamin Keen, pastor of a white church in Petersburg began to miss some of his members, he asked his deacons where they were. They said: "They're down the road at the Peachy Plantation, listening to Rev. John Jasper." Dr. Keen said, "Rev. Jasper? He can't be a minister. God never ordains Negroes."

Dr. Keen and three of his deacons went to a meeting at Rev. Jasper's church and saw some of their own church members in the meeting. When John Jasper saw them, he smiled warmly and said: "Look here, you white folk; don't get in the seats of the regular customers."

Ten minutes later, Dr. Keen and his deacons were in tears, praising God. Their negative attitude toward blackness faded into the background as they were uplifted by what Rev. Jasper had to say. Later Keen said, "Thank God! He does ordain Negroes!"

After the Civil War, John Jasper was the first black minister to organize a church in Richmond. Dr. Hatcher, a white man who pastored Grace Baptist Church in Richmond, attended Jasper's Sunday afternoon services on and off for more than 20 years. He later wrote a biography called, *John Jasper—The Unmatched Black Philosopher and Preacher.*

Hatcher describes Jasper's preaching like this:

> "He circled around the pulpit with his ankle in his hand; and laughed and sang and shouted and acted about a dozen characters within the space of three minutes. Meanwhile, in spite of those things, he was pouring out a gospel sermon, red hot, full of love . . . full of tenderness."

Describing another one of Rev. Jasper's sermons, Hatcher says:

> "Men sobbed and fell to the floor in abject shame, and frightened cries for mercy rang wild through the church. Possibly never a sweeter gospel note sounded . . . There were many white persons present, and they went away filled with a sense of the greatness and power of the Gospel."

In another passage, Hatcher says:

> "By this time, Jasper seemed glorified. Earth could hardly hold him. He sprang about the platform with a boy's alertness; he was unconsciously waving his handkerchief as if greeting a great conqueror; his face was streaming with tears; he was bowing before the Redeemer; he was clapping his hands, laughing, shouting and wiping the blinding tears out of his eyes. It was a moment of transport and unmatched wonder to everyone, and I felt as if it

could never cease."

During his years of ministry, John Jasper became an institution in Virginia. He became so identified with Richmond that the gavel used by the mayor was made from wood taken from John Jasper's home.

One of Jasper's sermons became so famous he preached it more than 250 times, in nearly every county and city in Virginia, including once before the Virginia General Assembly. He then made a tour of Baltimore, Washington, Philadelphia, and New York while preaching before many thousands of people, both black and white.

When he died in 1901, *The Richmond Times Dispatch* called Jasper "a man of deep convictions, a man with a purpose in life, a man who earnestly desired to save souls for Heaven." Eleven years later when his friend and biographer, Dr. Hatcher was dying, Hatcher whispered, "John Jasper, we're brothers now, and we'll live forever around the throne of God."

Jasper once said: "The iniquity of slavery can never be obliterated without the mind of Christ. Unaided human thinking at its highest, as seen in Aristotle, defends bondage on the grounds of race diversity. But the Man of Galilee took the slave by one hand and the owner by the other, set them face to face, and said, 'You are brothers.'"

A 3rd Grade Lesson on Racism through EYES

Color discrimination is almost impossible to

comprehend. That's especially true if your own color is the majority and hasn't been labeled as offensive (or distasteful, inferior, or inadequate) nor has a false, insulting definition of your own color used to continually justify mistreating you.

The day after Martin Luther King, Jr. was shot, some third-grade children in Riceville, a white town in Iowa, had some questions about his assassination and why it had happened. One boy asked: "They shot a King last night, Mrs. Elliott, why did they shoot that King?"

So, their teacher, Jane Elliott, answered their questions and led them in a discussion about race and discrimination. However, she could tell her students were still mystified and could not "internalize it." They had grown up in and were living in an all-white town in which both the concept and the experience of being discriminated against because of color was completely foreign to them.

Jane realized the only way she could help her students understand color discrimination was to let them experience it.

So, she asked her students if they would like to experience discrimination, so they could understand it better. The class, trying hard to understand King's assassination, said they would. So, Jane designed an exercise to do with her class based on eye color instead of skin color.

On the first day of the exercise, Jane told her class

they were going to change how they did things. She told them that for the day, blue-eyed children were going to be the most important children in the classroom. They would be given more time for recess and more food at lunch. All the blue-eyed children would also be allowed to sit in the front of the class and have the right to participate in class discussion. The blue-eyed students were encouraged not to play with the brown-eyed ones. She told the class only blue-eyed children could drink from the water fountain, but brown-eyed students had to use paper cups.

Brown-eyed children had to sit at the back of the class and couldn't participate in discussions. She also had the blue-eyed students put cloth collars on the brown-eyed ones, so they could be easily identified.

Jane made up some fake news to justify all those changes. She told the children that *melanin* causes blue eyes and it also makes people more intelligent. Throughout the day, Jane encouraged the children to think of the brown-eyed children as inferior.

By the end of the day, the blue-eyed students were openly insulting the brown-eyed ones. Also, the blue-eyed students were doing better on class assignments than the brown-eyed ones, while the performance of the brown-eyed students had declined.

The next day, Jane told her students she had made a mistake—it is really brown-eyed people who have more *melanin* and are smarter. So, she reversed the exercise. The results were the same in reverse.

However, on the second-day, the brown-eyed students didn't make fun of the blue-eyed ones as much as they had been made fun of by the blue-eyed children (probably because they now had a first-hand experience of color-based discrimination).

At the end of the second day, Jane told the students eye-color really has nothing to do with people's intelligence or equality. The students cried and hugged each other across the eye-color-divide. An all-white class had experienced what color-based discrimination feels like.

Afterwards, Jane had all the students write an assignment about the experience and the local paper published some of them. That article was picked up by the Associated Press and was distributed across the country. Soon Jane was invited to be a guest on national television shows and newspapers wrote stories about her and the blue eyes/brown eyes exercise. There was a heated national discussion about what she had done.

She began to repeat the exercise in professional training for adults. Eventually several documentaries were made about it.

Jane described her students experience like this: "They said, 'I found out what it felt like to be on the bottom, and I did not want to make anyone feel like that ever again.'"

> "We are constantly being told that we don't have racism in this country anymore, but most of the

people who are saying that are white. White people think it isn't happening because it isn't happening to them."—Jane Elliott

My Own Blue Eyes

I have blue eyes. I don't mind people pointing that fact out. But I sure wouldn't want people to say (or silently believe) my blue eyes have negative meaning about who I am as a person.

If blue-eyed people were widely considered to be inferior to people of other eye colors, that would be hard for me. If for centuries blue-eyed people had been seen as only fit for human trafficking and forced labor, if they had been bought and sold like animals, and tortured when they disobeyed; that would make it much harder for me to feel really good about my blue eyes.

If the human traffickers of blue-eyed people were seen as heroes and founding fathers of my country, that would be tough. If the traffickers of blue-eyed people like me had claimed to be Christian and tried to justify their abuse of blue-eyed people by using Scripture to say God had cursed all blue-eyed people to servanthood and slavery, that would make me feel even worse.

If when blue-eyed people were finally set free from slavery, after about 250 years of horrible cruelty, laws were passed to say they couldn't associate with people of another eye color nor could they vote, I'd feel really bad about that. Moreover, if those laws had been enforced by hooded terrorists and mob violence . . . I'd be very sad. If it took about 100 years after blue-eyed people were freed for them to finally be given legal protection and voting rights, I would be heart-broken it took so long to recognize people with my eye color as deserving of human rights.

Furthermore if about 50 years after that, unarmed blue-eyed men were commonly shot dead by the police and the percentage of blue-eyed people in prison was far greater than the percentage of any other eye color, I'd feel like the lies about blue eye color being inferior were still believed by my countrymen. After all that abusive history, every time I looked at my blue eyes, I'd feel bad about myself. How about the rest of you blue-eyed people? I've got to say this, even if brown-eyed people want me to say: "All lives matter," I'd still say, "Blue-eyed lives matter."

A Myth That Needs to Go

As we have seen, the concept of race was developed in the Western world during the 17th Century as an attempt to justify the terrible crimes that were being committed against Africans. The nominally Christian West needed a way to ease their conscience for forcibly taking human captives from Africa, putting them through the torturous Middle Passage of the Atlantic, and holding them and their descendants in life-long bondage and forced labor.

The African characteristics of a dark complexion and kinky hair were said to make them a different and inferior race than the Europeans. East Asians were also defined as another race because of their eye slant and skin tone.

We seem to be still stuck on the myth of race in our time. Every time we fill out a form we are asked to continue this myth by writing down our race. I get tired of it, so sometimes I check the *other* category or write in *human* for my race.

Our news reporters constantly refer to people by the shade of their skin. But this is a very slanted approach. I have never heard a reporter say: "A blue-eyed man robbed a convenience store last night." Why not?

Our society still uses the myth of race to define, separate, and marginalize people. Like the Pharisee in Jesus' parable, the concept of race allows us to look down on people and say (or think); "Thank God I'm not like them."

Isn't it time we erase the myth of race and embrace our shared humanity? Can we ever get beyond divisive classifications?

USA Government's Confusing "Racial" Categories

In 1977 the federal government introduced a list of human categories to more clearly define racial/ethnic groups, so they could be protected from discrimination. However, rather than creating color/cultural appreciation, their list seems to create color/cultural confusion.

Working for The Salvation Army, Ernie and I hired a lot of people, both black and white, as bell ringers. The government required us to ask every person to pick one of these categories for themselves, or sign a document declining to do so. Having to explain this list to several hundred people over the years, was always awkward, regardless of a person's color.

Here's the list:

>American Indian or Alaskan Native – "A person having origins in any of the original peoples of North and South America (including Central America), and who maintains tribal affiliation or community recognition."
>
>Asian – "A person having origins in any of the original peoples of the Far East, Southeast Asia, the Indian subcontinent, including for example, Cambodia, China, India, Japan, Korea, Malaysia, Pakistan, the Philippine Islands, Thailand, and Vietnam."
>
>Black or African American – "A person having origins in any of the black racial groups of Africa. Terms such as *Hattian* or *Negro* can be used in addition to *Black* or *African American*."
>
>Hispanic or Latino – "A person of Cuban, Mexican, Puerto Rican, or Central American, or other Spanish culture of origin, regardless of race. The term *Spanish origin* can be used in addition to *Hispanic or Latino*."

Native Hawaiian or Other Pacific Islander – "A person having origins in any of the original peoples of Hawaii, Guam, Samoa, or other Pacific Islands."

White – "A person having origins in any of the original peoples of Europe, the Middle East, or North Africa."

As you can see, the definitions of these groups are inconsistent.

- It's based on ancestry rather than physical characteristics.

- Except for black and white it doesn't mention skin color. Red, brown, and yellow skin are left out.

- Every group isn't classified the same way. For example, Native American is the only classification that requires "tribal affiliation or community recognition," and African American is the only category identified as being from "racial groups," while Hispanic or Latino is classified as of "Spanish culture of origin, regardless of race."

Alternative to Skin-Color Categorization – DISC

So, can we humans be aware of skin color without categorizing people by it? Of course, we can. We do that with eye color all the time. We notice people with blue eyes, but we don't separate ourselves from them or see them in anyway less than we are because of their eye color.

Skin complexion is an obvious human characteristic. We wear it all over our bodies. We may say that we are colorblind, but we still notice people's skin color; however, epidermis shading is not really a very accurate way to classify people, because people of any given skin-shade are as diverse as blue-eyed people are.

When we evaluate people by *RYBD* (red, yellow, black, and white) we miss the essence of who they are as individuals. The color of their skin tells us very little about their personalities.

Let's take a brief look at a more effective way to classify people. Ernie and I like to use a classification system called *DISC* based on an assessment instrument. The **D** stands for Dominant. This person is direct, determined, work oriented, and self-confident. They focus on getting a job done.

The **I** stands for Influencer. The **I** is warm, friendly, outgoing, and talkative. their focus is on meeting people, making lots of friends, and having fun while doing it. They are very optimistic.

The **S** stands for Steady. This person is loyal, calm, and a good listener. This person emphasizes teamwork and supporting others. They are very family focused.

The **C** stands for Compliant. The **C** is accurate, careful, analytical, and creative. Their focus is on correctness and getting the job done right.

Ernie has led hundreds of seminars based on the DISC Personal Profile and I've led quite a few. It is a document that contains a series of questions designed to help people discover their style. In the course of the seminar, we like to get people into small groups according to their style. Then we ask each group to discuss and answer a few questions about their style. They talk about their style's likes and dislikes.

It's fun to watch people's faces light up as they are suddenly surrounded by a small group of people who think and feel like they do. They sense almost immediate comradery and friendship.

Often, the people in the group are various colors. It's always amazing to see 3 blacks, 3 whites, 2 Hispanics, and an Asian (or some other color combination) stand up in front of the larger group, sometimes arm-in-arm as they talk about their style, saying; "We **Is** love people and for us the workplace needs to be fun!" Sometimes they even sing a song together.

Then a multi-colored group of **Ss** will get up and say something like: "We **Ss** can't work well if there is conflict in the office. We need everybody to get along and to support one another." In that moment, that group is no longer divided as black, white, or brown—they really do see themselves as a united brotherhood of **Ss**.

Next various colors of **Cs** will say: "We want the job done right. Just give us accurate information and don't waste our time with *fluff.*" The **Cs** will all be very serious as they share with the big group.

Finally, a rainbow of **Ds** will say: "Just do what we say and you will get along well with us."

Watching this I always wonder, what has skin color got to do with personalities and relationships? Complexional prejudice has no basis in fact. The truth is, each of us has far more in common with other people who are the same style as us than we do with other people who are the same color as we are. As Josephine Baker, an African-American who moved to France and became a popular entertainer there in the early Twentieth Century, said: "Surely the day will come when color means no more than skin tone."

(If you would like to know more about DISC and how to use it to help bridge color barriers, contact me at stsimms@live.com.)

As Angela Davis said:

"I am beginning to think that race is an increasingly obsolete way to construct community."

Perhaps *DISC* can help us move on.

10. Cash for Slaves & Priceless Courage

More of My Innovative Thoughts About Race

When society goes tribalistic, logic and love get lost in the uproar. It's so easy to let one person's negative behavior influence our opinion of an entire shade of humanity. We can't appreciate skin color if our mind and heart are lodged in the dark.

It's dangerous to think you have immunity to racism; that it's impossible for you to have racist thoughts or feelings. Do not let skin color be a camouflage keeping you from seeing the unique person living in the skin.

America's Forgotten Black *Trail Of Tears*

Before *Cash For Gold* and *Cash For Houses* ads became popular, *Cash For Slaves* ads were popular in certain places in America. That's because many slaveholders were selling their slaves to domestic American slave-traders to take advantage of the rising slave prices, driven by the growing demand for forced-laborers in the Cotton Belt of the Deep South. Slaves were selling for a lot more there than they were in the Upper South. So, domestic slave-traders would buy enslaved people in the Upper South and move them to the Deep South by either boat or by a 1,000-mile forced march.

The slaves called this being "sold down river." It is estimated that between the 1820s and the beginning of the Civil War, about a million human captives were forcibly driven or shipped to and resold into slavery in the Deep South.

Over land the slaves would travel in coffles. A coffle is defined as "a line of animals or slaves fastened or driven along together"—a traveling chain gang of innocent people. One of the largest slave-trading firms in America was Franklin and Armfield, owned and operated by infamous slaver, Isaac Franklin, of Gallatin, Tennessee. By the 1830s they were moving about 1,000 slaves a year to market in Natchez, Mississippi and New Orleans, by land and by sea.

Isaac Franklin personally led an annual coffle of about 400 slaves 1,000 miles over land. Every year he would drive his human chattel from Alexandria, DC (now part of Virginia) right by Fairvue, his personal plantation mansion in Gallatin, Tennessee (the largest one in Tennessee) and then herd them down Gallatin Road, right through Nashville; then continue down the 444-mile-long Natchez Trace to Natchez, Mississippi. Through this hideous, but legal and profitable "business," Franklin became one of the richest men in America.

During this 1,000 mile "trail of tears," men were usually manacled and chained together in double lines. To keep them in step, they were often forced to sing as they walked. Women also walked and were sometimes tied together with ropes. Anyone who didn't submit and cooperate was whipped.

Children and injured adults rode in wagons with the supplies. White men, armed with guns and whips, were employed to herd the captives and keep them moving. Today we cannot imagine the amount of sufferings these people who were forced to make that trip went through. However, the slaves themselves said the intense labor of being a slave in cotton country was even worse than the coffle that brought them there along the black trail of tears.

> "The Natchez Trace was possibly the most recent legal slave route in North America. From the 1830s through the Civil war, many thousands of bonds people were transported from the southeast (Maryland to Florida) to the 'new' lands of the old southwest (Mississippi and Alabama). The most efficient route for this was often the Natchez Trace where, at the end of their journey, they would be sold at the *Forks in the Road* slave market."—Natchez Trace Parkway literature

I had always thought the Natchez Trace had been an Indian trail and later a trade route. Now we know it was only part of the story. It was also an American human trafficking route for many thousands of slaves. A few days after writing this I went to the Birdsong Hollow parking area on Natchez Trace. When I drove there I saw only one car in the small parking lot. I didn't see any people.

I got out of my car and knelt by the side of the road and prayed. I asked God to forgive my nation for the horrible sin of marching many thousands of innocent people in chain gangs down this route to be sold into Deep South cotton field slavery. I asked God to let this evil be commonly known in our time.

As I looked toward Nashville, I imagined a large chain-gang of 400 black Americans marching two-by-two toward the Deep South with wagons following them. Then I got up and looked in the other direction and saw two young black women walking side by side, away from me and towards Mississippi. It was like my imagination stepped into reality. Suddenly another black woman came into my sight, carrying a skate board. She got on the skate board and rolled to catch up with the other two, like the wagons in my imagination. The things I'm describing in this book aren't fiction. They were done to real human beings, just like the ladies I saw walking down Natchez Trace today.

Charles Ball wrote a slave narrative called: *Slavery in the United States—A Narrative of the Life and Adventures of Charles Ball, a Black Man, Who Lived Forty Years in Maryland, South Carolina, and Georgia, as a Slave Under Various Masters* which was published in 1837. He was herded with several coffles before he was finally able to run away from slavery.

Once Ball was bought for resell by a slave trader on Maryland's Eastern Shore to be trafficked to the Deep South. He wrote:

> "I joined fifty-one other slaves whom he had bought in Maryland. Thirty-two of these were men and nineteen were women. The women were merely tied together with a rope, about the size of a bed cord, which was tied like a halter round the neck of each; but the men, of whom I

was the stoutest and strongest, were very differently caparisoned. A strong iron collar was closely fitted by means of a padlock round each of our necks. A chain of iron, about a hundred feet in length, was passed through the hasp of each padlock, except at the two ends, where the hasps of the padlocks passed through a link of the chain. In addition to this, we were handcuffed in pairs, with iron staples and bolts, with a short chain, about a foot long, uniting the handcuffs and their wearers in pairs. In this manner we were chained alternately by the right and left hand; and the poor man, to whom I was thus ironed, wept like an infant when the blacksmith, with his heavy hammer, fastened the ends of the bolts that kept the staples from slipping from our arms."

Charles Ball's Personal Account of Slavery

"My mother had several children, my brothers and sisters, and we were all sold on the same day to different purchasers. Our new masters took us away, and I never saw my mother, nor any of my brothers and sisters afterwards. This was, I presume, about the year 1785. I learned subsequently, from my father, that my mother was sold to a Georgia trader, who soon after that carried her away from Maryland. Her other children were sold to slave-dealers from Carolina, and were also taken away, so that I was left alone in Calvert county, with my father, whose owner lived only a few miles from my new master's residence. At the time I was sold I was quite naked, having never had any clothes in my life; but my new master had brought with him a child's frock or wrapper, belonging to one of his own children; and after he had purchased me, he dressed me in this garment, took me before him on his horse, and started home; but my poor mother, when she saw me leaving her for the last time, ran after me, took me down from the horse, clasped me in her arms, and wept loudly and bitterly over me . . . Young as I was, the horrors of that day sank deeply into my heart, and even at this time, though half a century has elapsed, the terrors of the scene return with painful vividness upon my memory."

Later he tells about how one of his masters had an overseer give him twelve lashes on his back and then had another slave pour scalding red-pepper tea into his wounds. Ball writes: "This operation was continued at regular intervals, until I had received ninety-six lashes, and my back was cut and scalded from end to end." Then he was hung by his thumbs for an hour and a half.

Was Jesus Whipped in America?

Millions of people around the world have seen the stunning and horrifying images of whipping and torture in the movie *The Passion of The Christ* produced by Mel Gibson. It is deeply moving to see what Jesus was put through in Jerusalem—even though Pilate declared: "I find no fault in him."

It is heart rending to see an innocent person viciously whipped. Jesus said:

"What you do to the least of these, my brothers, you do unto Me."

Who are "the least" in American history? Wouldn't that be the slaves who had no legal rights and were trafficked like animals? According to Jesus, what was done to the slaves, was done to Christ. Jesus was whipped in America.

> In 1848, **Frederick Douglas** said: "I am afraid you do not understand the awful character of the lashes given to slaves. A human being in a perfect state of nudity, tied hand and foot to a stake, and a strong man standing behind with a heavy whip, knotted at the end, each blow cutting into the flesh, and leaving the warm blood dripping to the feet." *Jesus was whipped in America.*

> *John Fee*, a white Kentuckian, wrote: "Let me say, the torture of the body is terribly cruel, and yet it is the smallest part of the crime of human slavery. I have seen women tied to a tree or timber and whipped with cow-hides on their bare bodies until their shrieks would seem to rend the very heavens." *Jesus was whipped in America.*

> **Absalom Jones**, a founder of the African Methodist Episcopal Church, said in the late 1700's: "Our God has seen masters, and mistresses, educated in fashionable life, sometimes take the instruments of torture into their own hands, and deaf to the cries and shrieks of their agonizing slaves, exceed even their overseers in cruelty." *Jesus was whipped in America.*

American poet, **John Greenleaf Whittier**, wrote about slavery in 1845: "Woe to him who crushes the soul with chain and rod, and herds with lower natures, the awesome form of God." *Jesus was whipped in America.*

Francis Fredric, himself once given 107 lashes, wrote in 1863: "I saw a slave flogged (for running away) in the presence of all the slaves assembled from the neighboring plantations. His body was frightfully lacerated. I went to see him two or three weeks after the flogging. When they were anointing his back, his screams were awful. He died soon afterwards–a tall, fine young fellow, six feet high, in the prime of life, thus brutally murdered." *Jesus was whipped in America.*

Solomon Northup, author of *Twelve Years A Slave,* wrote: "I thought I must die beneath the lashes of the accursed brute. Even now the flesh crawls upon my bones, as I recall the scene. I was all on fire. My sufferings I can compare to nothing else than the burning agonies of hell." *Jesus was whipped in America.*

Many want the story of the American Passion (of both black Americans and the original Americans) left untold. The violence we have done to Jesus–"to the least of these"–to those who have done us no wrong–is easier denied than faced. It is very humbling to realize the evil and the cruelty that was committed by our forefathers right here on American soil as they proclaimed, "liberty and justice for all." Lord, have mercy on us.

Negro Spirituals

> "Over my head I hear music in the air, there must be a God somewhere." –Negro spiritual.

Those words were written and sung during the most difficult of days, a time of great oppression and evil—a time of bondage, of fear, of violence, of economic deprivation, of disrespect, and of despair. Somehow, as they suffered from man's inhumanity to man, our African-American forefathers were able to discover and to express a strong hope in God.

"Over my head . . ." The millions of people being human trafficked in America had to look beyond themselves to find hope. Their mind and their emotions told them that their situation was hopeless—that their life was nothing but meaningless drudgery, suffering, and injustice. In order to survive, they had to look up, over their head, and get a different perspective. They had to tune their heart to hear "music in the air."

Although human beings have a sense of the eternal, an awareness that life is more than breathing in and out, many of us get so caught up in our personal pursuit of pleasure we don't hear the eternal music. Pain, however, can wake us up to truths that are over our head—beyond our intellect. It can cause us to hear melodies of mystery and meaning bringing insight and understanding.

"There must be a God somewhere." That revelation

gave the slaves Someone to hold on to. And even more, it gave them a faith Someone was holding on to them—a rock, a strength, an unshakable security—even in the midst of their suffering and struggles.

The American slaves found deep strength and comfort in the powerful truths of their abusers' religion. They heard the events of Scripture and discovered the holy and loving Jesus Christ, Who rescued the Bible people—He was still alive in their day and willing to reveal Himself in comfort to the despised and the downtrodden. That's why they sang. Negro spirituals declare God will come and help us if we cry out and seek Him with all of our heart.

Even when the slaves found Jesus, their tormentors refused to recognize them as equal brothers and sisters in Christ. They continued to look down on them. They wouldn't let them learn to read the Bible. They usually would not let them meet together for worship unless a white slave-holder or overseer was there to spy on them.

Most Americans believe there has never been widespread persecution of Christians in our country. But black Christians were continually persecuted. Until the middle of the twentieth century they were harassed, and their churches were actually bombed by whites.

Quotes from Quobna Ottobah Cugoano

Quobna Ottobah Cugoano was kidnapped and

tortured by human traffickers when he was 13 years-old and living in Africa in the late 1700s. He was taken to England and forcibly held against his will as a slave. (His slave name was *John Stuart.*) After experiencing much cruelty and suffering, he finally got his freedom and learned to read and write.

These quotations come from his book: *Thoughts And Sentiments On The Evil And Wicked Traffic Of The Slavery And Commerce Of The Human Species, Humbly Submitted To The Inhabitants Of Great Britain,* which was published in 1787.

> "I was brought from a state of innocence and freedom, and in a barbarous and cruel manner, conveyed to a state of horror and slavery."

> "How wonderful is the divine goodness displayed in the Old and New Testaments! O what a treasure to have and to be able to read therein."

> "Those men that are the procurers and holders of slaves are the greatest villains in the world. They must be lost to all sensibility, thinking that the stealing, robbing, enslaving, and murdering of men are not crimes."

> "If a man have not love in his heart for his fellow creatures, all his other virtues are not worth a straw."

> "The destroyers and enslavers of men cannot be Christians, for Christianity is the system of love, and its followers are devoted to honesty, justice,

humanity, meekness, peace, and good will to all men."

"Good soldiers of Jesus Christ have many battles to fight with their unbelief, with the perverseness of their nature, with evil temper, and with besetting sins."

Prime Shipping in Mr. Brown's Box

Henry Box Brown was born a slave on a plantation in Louisa County, Virginia, about 1815. In 1848 his wife and four children were sold to a man in North Carolina and forcibly hauled away. After that, Henry felt like he had nothing else to lose, so he decided he had to escape, no matter what. He prayed, and God gave him a plan.

Brown asked his friend James Caesar Anthony Smith, a free black, and a white man named Samuel Smith to help him escape by thinking inside the box. Smith actually put Brown inside a wooden crate and shipped him from Richmond, Virginia to the headquarters of the Philadelphia Anti-Slavery Society on March 23, 1849. The box was marked "dry goods." It had a hole in the top for air and was lined with cloth. It was three feet long, two feet deep and about two and a half feet wide. He had a few biscuits and a bottle of water with him.

In just 27 hours (overnight shipping) the box arrived. The Anti-Slavery activists were amazed when a hero for American freedom popped out of the box and sang these words from an Old Testament Psalm: "I waited patiently for the Lord;

And He, in kindness to me, heard my calling, And He hath put a new song into my mouth, Even thanksgiving unto our God." Brown always said that the escape plan came from what God told him, "Go and get a box and put yourself in it."

The Abolitionists were amaze from what God told him to do. God had delivered an escaped slave, right to their office. Soon afterwards, Brown was invited to speak before the New England Anti-Slavery Society in Boston where he told and performed the story of his escape which opened the door for him to speak at anti-slavery meetings around the region. A Boston publisher helped Brown write his story and published it in 1849. It became one of America's best-known slave narratives.

Brown was very creative and artistic. By 1850 he had produced a stage show named *Henry Box Brown's Mirror of Slavery*. It featured a huge canvas about 10 feet tall, which was slowly unrolled as Brown sang and spoke about his experiences. The canvas featured a panorama of 49 scenes picturing the things Henry endured as a slave. Soon afterwards the Fugitive Slave Act of 1850 was passed by Congress, requiring any American to report runaway slaves. Henry, realizing he could easily be recaptured if he stayed in America, went to England where he put on stage productions to tell the story of American slavery, as well as his personal bondage and liberation.

Here are some quotes from Henry Box Brown

"I now began to get weary of my bonds; and

earnestly panted after liberty. I felt convinced that I should be acting in accordance with the will of God, if I could snap in sunder those bonds by which I was held body and soul as the property of a fellow man. I looked forward to the good time which every day I more and more firmly believed would yet come, when I should walk the face of the earth in full possession of all that freedom."

"I entered the world as a slave—in the midst of a country whose most honored writings declare that all men have a right to liberty."

"I was a slave because my countrymen had made it lawful in utter contempt of the declared will of Heaven."

Underground Railroad

The Underground Railroad was a network of people, black and white, who led escaped slaves across various safe routes to freedom in the North and/or Canada. It operated from the late 1700s to the Civil War.

People who guided the runaway slaves were known as "conductors." They hid them along the escape route in various hiding places which included, people's homes, churches, schools, and even campsites. These were called *depots*, stations, or *safe houses*. The hosts who operated them were known as *stationmasters*.

The best-known conductor was Harriet Tubman.

Harriet was born a slave and given the name Araminta Ross. She was married to another slave named Tubman. After she escaped from slavery in 1849 she changed her name to Harriet. Harriet later risked her life to make trips back to the plantation in Maryland where she was born and rescue family members and other slaves. During her life, Harriet repeatedly made dangerous trips into the South to lead slaves to freedom.

In Northern states a *reverse Underground Railroad* developed. Slave hunters would search for suspected runaways, kidnap blacks (self-emancipated slaves and sometimes free blacks), and forcibly take them back to the South for reward money or to resell them into slavery. In Northern states that bordered the Ohio River, slave hunters often bound and hid blacks in homes, barns, or other buildings until they could be taken South into slavery.

Cash for Slaves and Priceless Courage

11. *Seeing More Clearly?*

Fresh Thoughts About Race

The light of Christ empowers us to see beyond society's myths, cultures, traditions, and our own personal opinions. Dare we see more clearly? The significant differences between groups of people aren't physical, but cultural. They aren't innate differences but learned differences.

The myth of race still lingers and hinders the heartfelt appreciation of people who look different than we do. Listening to a lecturer (or reading a book) isn't diversity training. Jumping into the middle of another culture is! To make diversity training a one-time event is like making breathing a one-time event.

Just because you know how to disagree with people of all colors, doesn't mean you are educated in diversity. When I just see and hang with people like me, there's no diversity!

Humanity is a tapestry of colors woven together; yet too often we focus on one color and try to ignore or exclude the rest. People, like the colored tiles in a mosaic, can compliment each other and work together to present a beautiful image.

It's easy to have a subconscious color guard against certain shades of people and not be aware of it. So, what is the normal skin color? There isn't one! Every skin color is unique.

You're brave. You can handle the truth. Thank you

for reading this far in my book!

Blame and Shame

There is plenty of room for both blame and shame about the many racial injustices of American history. Blacks and other minorities can get easily caught up with blame and anger. Whites are susceptible to shame. So, for both, it's often easier to ignore or whitewash the facts of history; to pull an oxymoron by attempting to justify past injustices and considering them no longer relevant to life today—politically incorrect—troublesome taboo.

However, as we have seen, the present was produced by the behaviors of the past and the beliefs about people who drove those past behaviors. Fortunately, many of the injustices of American history have been stopped, yet some of the beliefs which drove those behaviors are still with us—they still need to be refuted, rebuffed, and replaced.

Indeed, blame and shame won't heal the present-day pain of past racial injustice. Instead, they continually maim people making them lame and putting salt into their wounds. Then denial and defensiveness come along attempting to ease our pain by trying to bury blame and shame in forced forgetfulness, by ignoring, or disguising the injustices and beliefs behind them.

However, truth can set both blacks and whites free from blame and shame. The truth of exposing and renouncing false beliefs hidden in unjust behaviors of the past, can give us the ability to truly forge forward and blast past the pain of the past through healing and reconciliation.

One thing that helps get beyond racial blame is to separate things done to your ancestors from things actually done to you. You and they are not the same.

Another thing which helps get beyond racial shame is to separate things done by your ancestors from things actually done by you. You are not responsible for what they did.

Shoots and Roots

You can cut down some kinds of trees, but until the roots are pulled up and removed, those trees will keep sending out shoots. Racial problems are like those trees. To untangle society from today's racial roots, we do not need to be colorblind; instead, we need to unearth and expose our culture's racial roots.

Is it okay to ask this question? If someone you had greatly admired for years, as a good person and a hero, was caught running a human trafficking ring and proven to be guilty without any doubt—would you still consider him to be a good person, a hero?

I've never heard of a single black person who advocated blacks holding whites in slavery. However, what if there were a black man in American history who had actually held white people in slavery (and/or supported those who did)? What if a black mayor (and or city council) commissioned a statue of that black man who trafficked whites and had it set up in a prominent public place in your city? How would feel about that statue and that mayor or city council? Would you want the statue taken down?

Speaking of statues: Americans have set up many statutes to honor and remember whites who resisted the *tyranny* of being a British colony and led a violent rebellion for freedom against "taxation without representation." Why aren't there statues honoring and remembering the many blacks who resisted the tyranny of complexion-based human trafficking (like the heroic runaway slaves and the black Abolitionists)? Why aren't there statues honoring the black freedom fighters who led rebellions against life-long forced labor, abuse, and torture based solely on skin color (like Nat Turner)?

Today, there is a statue controversy in America. After the Civil War whites in the South began to erect statues of men who either owned slaves and/or defended the slave culture of the South, placing them in prominent places like courthouses and parks, where they mostly remain to this day. Many blacks and some whites are offended by those statues. If you were suddenly black (or have been black all your life) how would (do) you feel about those statues?

Injustice Hidden Behind the Bill Of Rights

The Bill of Rights is the first ten amendments to the U.S. Constitution. It originally was a list of protections for white Americans to enjoy. However, since at the time most blacks in America were considered to be property and not citizens or full human beings, for most black Americans the Bill of Rights was a *bill* of wrongs—a price most blacks were required to pay in full.

Here is my attempt to reveal the truth of how the Bill of Rights applied to blacks at the time of its writing and during the times of slavery. (Of course, many of these abuses continued after emancipation and were supported by Jim Crow laws that weren't struck down until the 1960s.)

First Amendment for White Americans:

> "Congress shall make no law respecting an establishment of religion, or prohibiting the free exercise thereof; or abridging the freedom of speech, or of the press; or the right of the people peaceably to assemble, and to petition the Government for a redress of grievances."

First Amendment as originally applied to most blacks:

> "Blacks will be prohibited from the free exercise of religion, especially the religion of their homeland. They shall not be allowed to learn to read any religious material, especially the Bible. They shall not be allowed to gather for worship without a white person present to monitor and control the meeting."

> "Blacks shall not be allowed any freedom to speak any of their own ideas, feelings, or

opinions; but shall be required to say whatever those whites exercising authority over them shall demand. Blacks will not be allowed to learn to read or write and therefore should have no freedom of the press."

"If blacks try to assemble on their own, they will be forcibly dispersed. Blacks will have no right to petition the Government or any other institution or individuals for a redress of grievances."

Second Amendment for white Americans:

"A well-regulated Militia, being necessary to the security of a free State, the right of the people to keep and bear Arms, shall not be infringed."

Second Amendment as originally applied to most blacks:

"Defenseless blacks being necessary to the security of slavery, blacks are not to be seen as people and therefore have no rights to any arms whatsoever. In fact, weapons of all kinds are to be kept away from them at all costs. They are to be in and to remain in a totally defenseless state."

Third Amendment for white Americans:

"No Soldier shall, in time of peace be quartered in any house, without the consent of the Owner, nor in time of war, but in a manner to be prescribed by law."

Third Amendment as originally applied to most

blacks:

> "If ever necessary, soldiers shall do whatever they are commanded to do in order to forcibly keep blacks in perpetual bondage, servitude, and subservience."

Fourth Amendment for white Americans:

> "The right of the people to be secure in their persons, houses, papers, and effects, against unreasonable searches and seizures, shall not be violated, and no Warrants shall issue, but upon probable cause, supported by Oath or affirmation, and particularly describing the place to be searched, and the persons or things to be seized."

Fourth Amendment as originally applied to most blacks:

> "Since blacks aren't officially people and their persons (in most cases) *belong* to a white *owner*; therefore, they have no right to be secure in anything. Their houses, and effects and even their bodies, are all solely the property of their master and can be violated at any time. They have no *papers* since they are not allowed to learn to read or write. Warrants are completely unnecessary and there is no need for probable cause. In fact, their blackness itself is probable cause they have already done something wrong, just by existing. They can be forcibly searched and seized at any time and in any place."

Fifth Amendment for white Americans:

> "No person shall be held to answer for a capital, or otherwise infamous crime, unless on a presentment or indictment of a Grand Jury and except in cases arising in the land or naval forces, or in the Militia, when in actual service in time of War or public danger; nor shall any person be subject for the same offence to be twice put in jeopardy of life or limb; nor shall be compelled in any criminal case to be a witness against himself, nor be deprived of life, liberty, or property, without due process of law; nor shall private property be taken for public use, without just compensation."

Fifth Amendment as originally applied to most blacks:

> "Blacks being personal property, not properly *persons*, shall be held to answer for a capital or otherwise infamous crime (whether real or imagined) without any knowledge of a Grand Jury, regardless of the case. Their master may abuse, torture, rape, and even kill them (whether they have committed a crime or not). They may be put in jeopardy of life or limb as many times as their master may desire. They will always be required (and forced if they refuse) to witness against themselves and against one another. They have no access to any due process of law. Since most blacks are private property (and have already been deprived of life, liberty, and property), they cannot be taken from their master for public use (like building the U.S.

Capitol) without just compensation paid to their master."

Sixth Amendment for white Americans:

"In all criminal prosecutions, the accused shall enjoy the right to a speedy and public trial, by an impartial jury of the State and district wherein the crime shall have been committed, which district shall have been previously ascertained by law, and to be informed of the nature and cause of the accusation; to be confronted with the witnesses against him; to have compulsory process for obtaining witnesses in his favor, and to have the Assistance of Counsel for his defense."

Sixth Amendment as originally applied to most blacks:

"Since most blacks are property, they have no more right to a public trial than livestock. There is no need to waste the time of a jury. Besides, blacks are not allowed to testify in a trial anyway. There is also no need for Counsel because there is no allowable defense for their insubordinate and rebellious behavior."

Seventh Amendment for white Americans:

"In suits at common law, where the value in controversy shall exceed twenty dollars, the right of trial by jury shall be preserved, and no fact tried by a jury, shall be otherwise re-examined in any court of the United States, than according to the rules of the common law."

Seventh Amendment as originally applied to most blacks:

> "As property, blacks have no right to common law or trial by jury, no matter what is done to them. The courts of the United States are not available to them."

Eighth Amendment for white Americans.

> "Excessive bail shall not be required, nor excessive fines imposed, nor cruel and unusual punishments inflicted."

Eighth Amendment as originally applied to most blacks:

> "Blacks can be held in lifelong bondage (and their generations after them) and their master can demand any excessive price he wants for them and turn down any price offered. He is allowed to inflict as many cruel and unusual punishments upon them as he desires . . . even to the point of death."

Ninth Amendment for white Americans:

> "The enumeration in the Constitution, of certain rights, shall not be construed to deny or disparage others retained by the people."

Ninth Amendment as originally applied to most blacks:

"Although white people may claim other rights that are not listed in the Constitution, blacks aren't considered to be people and therefore aren't allowed to claim any rights, whether listed in the Constitution or not."

Tenth Amendment for white Americans:

"The powers not delegated to the United States by the Constitution, nor prohibited by it to the States, are reserved to the States respectively, or to the people"

Tenth Amendment as originally applied to most blacks:

"Since blacks are not mentioned in the Constitution (except for the disguised mention in the 3/5 clause, where they are counted as 3/5 of a person, solely to increase the representation in Congress of the states where they are being held in slavery), the state blacks live in and the people of that state, may do anything they desire to their black population."

Dodging Slavery And Racial Injustice?

If you begin to talk to people about what you have learned in this book, many people will try to dodge the conversation. When I bring up the subject of slavery or racial injustice, most black people are ready to talk with me about it; however, many white people seem to prefer to dodge the subject. Here are some common verbal dodges:

❖ "Slavery wasn't that bad because the slaves were well treated."

Is being owned, treated like cattle, totally controlled, and forced to work without pay or any hope of escape, being well treated?

❖ "Slavery is in the past – it's over – so we don't need to think about it today."

Well, by definition, all history is over, done, and in the past; but people still like to study it, read novels about it, watch movies about it, and even celebrate their favorite parts of it. If we can talk about the inspirational parts of American history, why should we be silent about the unseemly parts?

❖ "Slavery was legal and therefore it was okay to hold slaves."

Can a government make something right by simply declaring it to be legal? Of course not. Throughout history (and even today) governments have legalized many unjust and immoral practices. There is a higher law than the laws of human governments—it is the law of God.

❖ "The men who held or used slaves were victims of their times. Today we know that slavery is wrong, but in their time, people didn't realize that."

But that's just not true. Many people, both white and black, spoke out about the cruelty and immorality of slavery for the entire 250 years it existed in North America. Even Thomas Jefferson, who personally held 200 innocent people in lifelong labor and bondage, knew it was wrong and wrote because of slavery, he trembled for our country when he remembered God is just. The founders of the United States were bright men. They knew slavery was wrong, but they chose to practice it and/or legalize it, despite its immoral practice.

> ❖ "There is no one alive today who owned slaves. We didn't have anything to do with it; so, we don't need to think about it."

Well there is also no one alive today who had anything to do with the Revolutionary War, writing The Declaration of Independence, ratifying the Constitution, the Civil War, etc., but we like to talk about them anyway. If we glory in and feel good about our country's past accomplishments, we personally had nothing to do with; why shouldn't we also admit and feel sorry about our country's wrongs we personally had nothing to do with? Isn't it a double standard to proudly celebrate the things we like in our history and then tell people who mention the evil in our history: "That's in the past—I had nothing to do with it."?

> ❖ "American blacks have benefited financially from their slave past because today they are the richest group of people of African descent in the world."

Let me ask you this: If someone murders a loved one of yours and you get rich off insurance money because of it, does that financial pay-off change the wickedness of the murder? Of course not. Just because someone benefits financially from evil, doesn't make it right.

Try not to be discouraged by the dodges. Continue to think about slavery and racial injustice. American slaves were awesome people who endured horrible abuse and yet, even against impossible odds, never gave up, and never stopped resisting. Many escaped slaves wrote those *slave narratives*, autobiographies about their lives in slavery. Those writings, though heart rending, are very enlightening and inspirational. Many free blacks risked their lives to write brilliant anti-slavery articles and books. Those men and women, the black abolitionists, are some of the bravest people in American history.

To learn the uncensored details about slavery is to see human nature at its worst. It is to grieve and cry with the victims of our land of liberty. But it is also to see how human beings can endure, overcome, and change, even under the most difficult circumstances imaginable.

Common Pictures In American Wallets & Purses

Have you ever thought about the pictures you carry in your purse or wallet? We Americans carry pictures of men who refused to let children go to school. The men in our wallets forced people to work and refused to pay them. They took children away from their parents and never let them get back together again. Men in our purses refused to let

Christians read the Bible or to go to the church of their choice.

Men in our purses complained about the King of England who was treating them badly. They said they had a right to take up arms against him. They called the king a *tyrant* for taxing their tea while they themselves claimed to *own* other human beings. They said the king had no right to tax them *without representation*, while they demanded their *right* to buy, sell, and abuse people while denying them any chance for freedom.

Men in our wallets wrote and signed beautiful documents declaring the *God-given* rights of man. They boldly declared *all men are created equal*, while they themselves forcibly held men, women, and children in lifelong bondage. Men in our purses wrote a beautiful *Bill of Rights* and then proceeded to deny those rights to one out of every five Americans.

The men in my wallet puzzle me. How did they proclaim freedom while actively engaging in human trafficking? Historian John Hope Franklin wrote:

> "One may well be saddened by the thought that the author of the *Declaration of Independence* and the commander of the Revolutionary Army and so many heroes of the Revolution were slaveholders. Even more disheartening, if such is possible, is that those same leaders and heroes were not greatly affected by the philosophy of freedom which they espoused."

Today we honor some of the founders of our

country with their pictures on our money. Those men produced a system of government bringing freedom to millions; yet most of the men on our money practiced the worst kind of cruelty to their fellow human beings on their plantations and seemed to hardly notice it. Theirs is a dual legacy— one of freedom and the other of tyranny and torture. No wonder our nation has always been and continues to be greatly disturbed about skin color!

After Charleston Black Church Shooting?

I've discovered a heart-bonding that is even stronger than family and far more powerful than color—it's my deep inner connection with people who passionately love, follow, and obey the living, resurrected Jesus Christ! Wherever they are in this world, whatever they look like, whatever church they belong to (or don't belong to), they are my brothers and sisters in Christ and I have an instant, heart-felt relationship with them.

When I heard about a young white man's vicious attack on and murder of my innocent brothers and sisters at Emanuel AME Church in Charleston, South Carolina after they welcomed him (although he was a stranger to them) into their participatory Bible study and warmly listened to his comments; it broke my heart and brought me to tears several times. To target a church for mass murder is extreme anti-Christian persecution!

A day after the AME church shootings, I did a "Christian magic show" for about 25 black 6 and 7-year old children. They clapped, laughed at, and were inspired by my illusions, but I was so sad to know they had heard (or would soon hear) about a white man who murdered black Christians. I cried.

Ernie just asked me what I am writing. So, I read it to her and cried all the way through it. "Weep with those who weep." That's not difficult for me to do. I wish I could do more to bring about healing in our nation. That's one reason I write. I want people to know there is supernatural healing, racial reconciliation, forgiveness, and transformation though the living Jesus.

As we have seen, because of our history, our natural eyes can easily be offended or frightened when they see someone with black skin color. However, when spiritual eyes see black skin color, they see amazing human beings, many who have wounded hearts. Everyone, like the prodigal son, needs to abandon skin-offense and to return to their Father's love. There's no other answer for violence, racism, insecurity, fear, deception, loneliness, or addiction.

Shortly after the AME church shooting, I learned about Marcus Stanley, an African-American brother in Christ who (like me) was transformed by the living resurrected Jesus. Marcus is a Virginia-based singer who in 2004 was shot 8 times, at point-blank range, while performing. He miraculously survived, but while attempting to deal with the pain and hurt, Marcus got addicted to pain medication and heroin. In 2010 Marcus went into a faith-based rehab and through the power of the living, resurrected Jesus Christ he was set free from his addiction and forgave the person who shot him. Today he is a

Gospel singer who travels world-wide sharing his story of how he found Christ and how he forgave the person who shot him and almost took his life.

When Marcus heard about the shootings at the Charleston AME church, he went to the shooter's Facebook page and posted these words:

> "I don't look at you with the eyes of hatred, or judge you by your appearance or race, but I look at you as a human being that made a horrible decision to take the lives of 9 living and breathing people. Children do not grow up with hatred in their hearts. In this world we are born colorblind. Somewhere along the line you were taught to hate people that are not like you and that is truly tragic. You have accomplished nothing from this killing, but planting seeds of pain that will remain forever in the hearts of the families that lost their lives and countless hearts around the country. If you are still out there and have your phone with you . . . Give your heart to Jesus and confess your sins with a heart of forgiveness. He is the only one that can save your soul and forgive you for the terrible act you have done. I love you Dylann… even in the midst of the darkness and pain you have caused, but more importantly, He loves you. If you would like to make that confession, then repeat these words . . ." (Marcus ends his comment to the shooter with prayer asking Jesus for forgiveness and salvation.)

Marcus explained his comment with these words:

> "A lot of people are going to be mad at me for doing this. But we react too quickly with hatred instead of getting to the root of the problem. So, I was reaching out to him not in hatred but in love."

He also said:

> "I'm on a movement for Christ and I'm not slowing down. Throw the stones, shoot the arrows, bad mouth me. I'm ready for whatever! I'm taking up my cross and I'm walking for the Lord. If I can change, anyone can change. My destiny is so much greater than music. Music is just a tool to reach where words fail. Let God use you any way that He can. Be an instrument."

I was also deeply touched by how the survivors of the shooting spoke to the demonized, white shooter in court and publicly forgave him. That's not only an amazing thing. It's supernatural.

Perhaps it is time to admit human trafficking was just as evil in the 18th Century as it is in the 21st Century! Dare we acknowledge many of the famous founders of our nation were just as evil as present-day human traffickers? The skin color of America's Founding Fathers' victims did not justify or excuse their crimes against humanity! Remember Robert Carter III (from chapter three)? He freed all of his slaves, more than 400 people. The other Founding Fathers could have done that as well.

All lives matter to God (and to me)—black/white, postnatal/prenatal, liberal/conservative, mean/nice, Democrat/Republican and any other dichotomy used to label the epitome of God's creation–human beings! Let's care for all humanity!

Apology

Once I was praying in an unknown tongue when my words suddenly changed to what sounded like an African language and to an intensity I've seldom experienced. I began to feel extreme agony and despair, like I never had felt before. It was so tormenting I fell over on the floor and curled up in a fetal position as the African sounding words continued to flow out of me.

After a few minutes the words changed back into a more familiar tongue. In my mind I asked; "Lord, what was that?"

In a flash God showed me I had been praying a prayer that had been prayed by an African slave while chained in the crowded and filthy cargo hold of an American bound slave ship. I began to sob uncontrollably.

God gave me a momentary glimpse of some of the evils and horrors my ancestors did to Africans, just because they had black skin. Afterwards the Holy Spirit urged me to write an apology.

I struggled with the idea for a while, because I don't represent any organization or government having anything to do with slavery, its evils, or its cruel aftermath. So, I couldn't speak for anybody but myself. But I stepped beyond my intimidation and wrote this:

> I apologize to all my fellow Americans who are black for all the pain, cruelty, and horror your forefathers have suffered at the hands of my forefathers. I am deeply sorry for the extreme evil perpetrated on your parents, your grandparents, and on all the various generations of your lineage.
>
> I apologize for slavery and all the evils which came out of it, for generations of white terrorism, for Jim Crow laws, for forced segregation, for "separate but equal," for racial slurs, for hatred, for discrimination, and for institutional structures continuing injustice.
>
> As a white teenager in the 1960s I thought segregation was wrong, but I did and said nothing. During the Civil Rights Movement I never marched or rode on a freedom bus or sat-in at a lunch counter or encouraged those who did. I was comfortable in my own little world. I am sorry I was so unaware and passive and colorblind to your pain and suffering. Please forgive me.
>
> I also apologize for all you have personally suffered from American color prejudice—for all the attacks on your self-esteem. I apologize for all

the jobs you have been denied because of your skin color. I am sorry for all the times you have seen your parents, children, or grandchildren mistreated because of their color.

I apologize for the times you are followed around by suspicious retail store clerks or stopped by suspicious cops because your skin happens to be black. I am sorry for racial profiling. I apologize for all the injustices done and said to you that I, as a white person, have no firsthand knowledge or understanding.

I pray this apology, although weak and imperfect, will be of help to you. There is no justification for the evils perpetrated upon you. You and your ancestors didn't deserve to be treated cruelly and harshly.

I am so grateful for all the many positive and uplifting experiences I have had with black Americans (of many types—from professionals to people hanging out on the streets) in my life. You have always treated me kindly, respectfully, and lovingly.

The more I hang out with my old black friends and new black friends, the more I see your perspective. Thank you for letting me into your lives.

Say it: "Black Lives Matter" & Why?

> In its early years America said
> That black lives don't matter

By subjecting millions of black lives to:
Human trafficking and abuse;
Lifelong bondage and work without pay;
Cruel separation from their families;
And brutal whippings if they didn't obey.
Then America set black lives "free"
And turned them over
To a cruel system of separation
That denied their newly bestowed
Constitutional rights through:
Ongoing name calling, social abuse,
Unjust laws, harassment, bullying,
Torture, murder, and terror;
Resulting in the illegal lynching
Of more than 4,000 black lives,
While authorities turned their backs
(Or even assisted in the evil)
And the US Congress
Refused to make a resolution against it
And to say that black lives matter.
Today it's way past time to
Show genuine color-kindness
By shouting it from the housetops,
And writing it on all of our hearts,
That black lives matter
Every bit as much
As white lives do!

Practical Steps to Color-Kindness

I asked several diverse people if they would answer a question for this book:

"How can we solve America's racial problems?"

Here are some of the responses I received. A few I have edited for length, but I've tried very carefully not to change the meaning of what they wrote. I really appreciate their input and value various viewpoints. I hope you do too.

Enoch, 62, black male, pastor:

> "The worst mistake made about race and diversity is to say, 'I don't see color.' However, this is usually said only in reference to blacks, while a distinction is made for other ethnicities like Jews, Hispanics, Latinos, etc. We need to embrace God's diverse creation and come out of denial regarding race. Of course, you see color. You see beauty in the rainbow and in flowers of various colors. How can you not see the color in diverse people?"

Joe, white male, Commissioner, The Salvation Army:

> "Racism is pervasive, a product of the sin nature. The solution is two-fold: prevention and purity. The Scriptures are clear: *'Train up a child in the way he should go, and when he is old he will not depart from it'* (Proverbs 22.6). Reaching a child in those formative years and instilling a pure heart is a Gospel imperative. "*. . . love one another fervently with a pure heart*" (1 Peter 1:22). And in this, the church is failing, and I dare say, at the root of the problem!"

Myron, black male:

"For one thing, black and white people (the majority) have no real clue of the history of black people and why they were treated in such an inhumane way. Open forums where people listen to one another to learn from each other with an ear to hear, are important. We need to want to understand, to want to listen to someone else's point of view."

Lisa, white female:

"I don't believe this will end it, but it might be a start—to start looking the problem straight in the eye."

Felicia, 56, black female:

"We have to be intentional about meeting together and discussing and praying about race relations or it will never happen. In Mississippi where I am from an organization called Mission Mississippi has worked to do just that—encouraging people of different races to do things together, socially."

Jeremy, 43, white male, counselor/writer:

"Racism in America will never be solved if we cannot first solve it in the church. Since racism is a sin, we cannot expect the world to solve their problem of sin unless it is first modeled by those who follow Jesus. So, answering the question of how to solve racism in America begins with how to solve racism in the church. And there is one main thing the church can practice which will go a long way toward this goal. We must practice radical, shocking, outrageous, scandalous grace. Since racism is a sin issue, the only way to solve any sin issue is with grace."

James, black male, pastor:

"As things sit right now I can think of no strategy or plan or program that has a possibility of bringing racial unity to the United States of America. The only thing that has any chance of working and if it's working it will work, is a supernatural, undeniable Act of the Holy Ghost. God will have to directly intervene in the affairs of men to change the racial climate, and racial equity and justice that has so far eluded our country. I actually see so little hope, outside of a move of God, for this situation that I am ashamed to acknowledge that it is this bad. That said, when the U.S. slaves needed deliverance Abraham Lincoln came on the scene. When Jim Crow ran rampant Martin Luther King arrived and organized the Montgomery Bus Boycott that changed the face of America for a season. And how can we forget when the children of Israel needed deliverance, Moses arrived."

Cecilia, black female, 55:

"To solve the problem of race in America, we must be consistent and persistent in our fight to overcome it. It will take individuals engaged in one-on-one relationships who embrace the concept of positivity and nonjudgmental approaches towards the person who holds racist views and behaviors. It will take being educated on the subtle ways that racism plays a part in every sector of society. And finally, those who say they have the answer to society's ills would have to confront their biases concerning racism and then truly be the answer."

Here are a few ideas of my own for solving America's racial problems:

- Read and research America's hidden history. (I got you started, now keep going.) Seek to find the truth, not just what makes you feel good or makes your race look good. Let it touch and break your heart, whatever your color.

- Learn and tell all sorts of American stories. Don't just tell the pleasant ones making you or your color look good but also share the painful ones, the ones that break your heart.

- Build equal, non-hierarchical relationships, both giving and receiving, with people who are of a different complexion than you.

- Talk with people of a different complexion about your experience of racism (or the lack thereof). Ask them about their experience of racism and listen compassionately, empathetically, and nonjudgmentally.

- Be bold and speak up against any negative, racial statements about people of another skin color.

- Intentionally find things to appreciate about people of different shades of skin. Learn to enjoy their culture.

- Forgive. Forgive and let go of any racial slights or wrongs that you (or someone you love) have ever received. To forgive is to give up any right you think you have to hold something against someone or against a group of people.

- Ask God to show you any racial sins and/or prejudices of your own. Don't try to justify them but admit them to God. Ask for God's forgiveness and resolve to leave your sins and prejudices behind.

- Openly admit the racial sin of America, don't try to hide it in order to protect your race. Bring it to the light. Forgive, but don't excuse, all the people in American history who have committed great abuse and cruelties based on skin color.

- Begin to honor all the people in American history (regardless of their complexion) who spoke against and fought against racial cruelty. My Top 10 Greatest Americans is a good place to start.

- Meet with a racially diverse group of people and use one of the stories in this book as a discussion topic.

Here's a good discussion starter: If someone offered you $20 million to let them permanently change your skin color, would you accept? Which color would you pick? Why?

Seeing More Clearly

12. A Few Encouraging Quotes

Thank you for staying with this book until the end. However, this is really just the beginning – a new beginning for you with some fresh insight and understanding. May you be color-kind everywhere you go! Here are a few closing quotes to help encourage you.

"One of the less dismaying aspects of race relations in the United States is that their improvement is not a matter of a few people having a great deal of courage. It is a matter of a great many people having just a little courage."—**Margaret Halsey**, 1946

"The practice of peace and reconciliation is one of the most vital and artistic of human actions."—**Nhat Hanh**

"We may have different religions, different languages, different colored skin, but we all belong to one human race."—**Kofi Annan**

"When there is teamwork and collaboration, wonderful things can be achieved."—**Mattie Stepanek**

"Alone we can do so little; together we can do so much."—**Helen Keller**

"As mankind is all one family, the rule of loving our neighbor as ourselves, extends to the performances of all duties of kindness to persons of all nations and all conditions of men."—**Noah Webster**

"True beauty is a warm heart, a kind soul, and an attentive ear." –**Ken Poirot**

"If there is to be reconciliation, first there must be truth."—**Timothy B. Tyson**

"It's not our differences that divide us. It is our inability to recognize, accept, and celebrate those differences."—**Andre Lorde**

"To pray together . . . is the most tender brotherhood of hope and sympathy that men can contract in this life." –**Madame de Stael**

"Reconciliation always brings a springtime to the soul."—**Brother Roger**

"When you're having what you feel like is a 'bad day' and then someone comes along out of nowhere and extends to you the simplest of kind gestures, you feel it so deeply within your heart."—**Miya Yamanouchi**

"We all live with the objective of being happy; our lives are all different and yet the same."—**Anne Frank**

"Divest me of every prejudice, unfriendly to the bond of brotherhood, which ties man to man.— **Beriah Green**, 1836

"When one has seen something of the world and human nature, one must conclude, after all, that between people in like stations of life, there is very little difference the world over."—**James Weldon Johnson**

A Few Encouraging Quotes

"It is never too late to give up your prejudices."—**Henry David Thoreau**

"Try going out of your comfort zone and doing something for someone else."—**Henry Hon**

"Cooperation builds community."—**Akiroq Brost**

REVIEWS

"Despite the many changes, our nation still struggles with racism and its legacy. Steve Simms walks us bravely through our dark history of slavery, while managing to do so with warmth and grace. He introduces us to unsung heroes, points out the faults of those we have long idolized, and ultimately paints a picture full of color and wonder and love. This is a book that should be read by everyone. It is a vital clanging of the bell, a wake-up call, and points us toward the power of love which can change generations to come. Simms writes with unsurpassed passion and grace"

Eric Wilson, New York Times bestselling author of *Fireproof and Facing the Giants*

"The racial divide in America is real and it is deep. Steve Simms begins his exploration of the problem with three questions. He then takes the reader on his personal journey into lives and circumstances that too few would even dare imagine going. He is intentional about finding answers—no matter the risks. But he cannot question without engaging experiences that would otherwise be unknown and thus unappreciated. This is a rare account of a man who literally takes action on his belief in the worth of others. Interested in discovering what you can do to address the problem? Then you must read Steve's story!"

Commissioner Israel L. Gaither
Retired USA National Commander
The Salvation Army, USA

Off the RACE Track

Made in the USA
Columbia, SC
14 October 2018